Glacier de Gebrulaz and Aiguille de Polset from the Col du Soufre

WALKING IN TH   ...AISE AND
BEAUFORTAIN ALPS

WALKING IN THE TARENTAISE AND BEAUFORTAIN ALPS

by

J.W.Akitt

CICERONE PRESS

MILNTHORPE, CUMBRIA

ISBN 1 85284 181 8
© J.W. Akitt 1995

A catalogue record for this book is available from the British Library

ACKNOWLEDGEMENTS

I wish to acknowledge the many people who have helped
me collect the material for this guide.

First and foremost is my wife Jean, who accompanied me
on many of the walks and who has helped me correct the
typescript, an invaluable but tedious job. Many others
accompanied me at different times: my son Neil, his wife
Jayne, Douglas Morrison, accompagnateurs Guy and Henri
from Bourg St Maurice, leaders of various outings organised
by the Tarentaise section of the Club Alpin Français, and
Nigel Percival and Audrey who discovered the book *Alpine
Partisan*, which helped to fill in my knowledge of the region.
To all these I give my heartfelt thanks.

ADVICE TO READERS

Readers are advised that whilst every effort is taken by the authors
to ensure the accuracy of this guidebook, changes can occur which
may affect the contents. A book of this nature is more prone to
change than a more general guide. Waymarking alters and there
may be new buildings or eradication of old buildings. It is advisable
to check locally on transport, accommodation, shops etc. Even
rights of way can be altered, paths can be eradicated by landslip,
forest clearances or changes of ownership. The publisher would
welcome notes of any such changes.

Front cover: The upper part of the Evettes glacier and the ice walls below
the Albaron on the right, from the Refuge des Evettes

CONTENTS

Walk grade(s) given in parentheses

CHAPTER 1: AROUND THE COL DE LA MADELEINE

PREFACE

It is some 14 years since my wife and I first started to walk the hills of this part of the Alps in summer. There seemed to be little information available and it soon became evident that the only way to find out if a track was practicable for the car, or if there was or was not a footpath in a particular place, was to go and see for ourselves. In this way we built up the information contained in this guide. Things have also changed considerably here during this time as walking has become more popular away from the traditional summer resorts. The paths are now much more used and signposts are springing up everywhere to help guide the visitor, to the extent that it has been impossible to keep abreast of all the latest improvements.

The opportunities for walking here are almost limitless. I describe 53 walks of a day's duration and 4 tours of 2, 3, 4 and 8 days' duration. There remain a few that I would have liked to include but one poor summer prevented me doing this, as well as breaking most of the rules regarding the normal behaviour of the weather, set out in the introduction. Nevertheless, I hope that the present offering will satisfy most people. In addition, for the not so fit or the not so young, I have described some 40 short walks at relatively low altitudes which take you to some very pleasant places in the mountains or among the high hamlets of the hillsides.

I wish to point out that the routes described in this guide are by no means the only walks possible in the areas chosen. The adventurous walker will see that some of the itineraries can be interlinked to make different tours. The mobile camper, in particular, should not find it too difficult to be creative. Whichever walks you do, I hope you enjoy this marvellous scenery and come to love the region as much as my wife and I do.

Séez, March 1995

Pays sauvage, aux abîmes vertigineux
Gorges profondes, et torrents déchâinés
Brusqu'avalanches, et nombreux villages sinistrés
Rugueuse et dure, Tarentaise vallée de nos aïeux

Tarentaise, tes altières montagnes enneigées
Nous donnent tant, si l'on sait les aimer
Moments intenses, privilèges de se surpasser
Plaisir solitaire, ou joie profonde a pouvoir partager

First and last verses from the song *Ma vieille vallée* by Jean Pierre Sardino, with permission.

An English version of this might be:

Wild, untamed country of breathtaking chasms
Deep gorges and unleashed torrents
Sudden avalanches, so many stricken villages
Rugged and hard, the valley of our forebears

Tarentaise, your lofty, snow covered mountains
Give us so much, if we know how to love them
Intense moments, opportunities to surpass ourselves
Solitary pleasure or the sharing of a deep joy

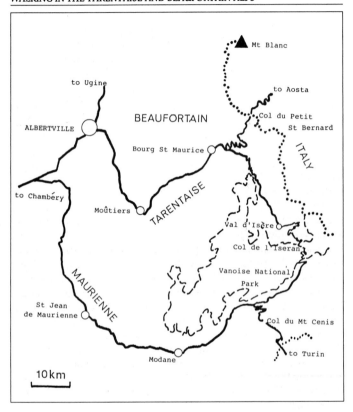

MAP 1. The Hen of Savoie, showing principal towns and roads and the names of the main regions discussed. The Franco-Italian border is shown dotted and follows a continuous mountain ridge. The complex shape of the Vanoise National Park is shown by a dashed line and extends to the border with Italy where it is contiguous with the Park of the Gran Paradiso. Mt Blanc has been also included to help place the region

INTRODUCTION

This book has been written to introduce British fellwalkers, indeed all English-speaking hillwalkers, to the region that lies mostly in France to the south of Mt Blanc. The area is little known outside France and yet provides a wealth of walks of varied nature among very attractive scenery. It is a relatively quiet part of the Alps and on some of the walks described it is unusual to meet more than a handful of people, if that. Nothing is described that could be regarded as mountaineering, though it is to be hoped that climbers may find some of the expeditions interesting, as possible alternatives to the higher hills when these suffer bad weather.

The area to be covered corresponds approximately to the eastern part of the department of Savoie. The nearest big town is Albertville, which was the centre for the 1992 Winter Olympic Games. The valley layout is complex, as a glance at the map will show. The main roads, which effectively show the position of the main valleys, outline a hen, known as *la Poule de Savoie*, with its beak pointing into the broad, flat valley to the west, which is called *la Combe de Savoie*. The belly of the hen forms the long, curving valley of the Maurienne, and the neck, back and tail feathers the M-shaped Tarentaise valleys. These names are of ancient origin going back at least to Charlemagne (in 800A.D.) and, surprisingly, the principal rivers bear different names from the valleys, the Arc in the Maurienne and the Isère in the Tarentaise. Thus the name Val d'Isère refers to a well known ski village at the head of the Tarentaise valley, not to the valley itself.

The Beaufortain lies to the north of the Tarentaise and shares its watershed. (There is some dispute as to the correct spelling of Beaufortain. The locals are sure that Beaufortain is correct but Beaufortin will also be encountered.) Part of the Tour of Mt Blanc long-distance footpath passes through this district. Italy lies to the east and is connected by roads over the Col du Petit St Bernard (known to the Romans as the Col Alpis Graia) or over the Col du Mt Cenis. In addition, there are seven cols which can easily be crossed on foot into Italy south of Mt Blanc. The popularity of the area for summer holidays has possibly suffered because it is sandwiched between the two high and prestigious mountain massives of Mt Blanc and the Dauphiné Alps and because many visitors have limited themselves to the winter season. Indeed, in winter the Tarentaise is a skiers' paradise and the economy of the region has been transformed by the so-called "white gold". This means, of course, that ski uplift equipment is visible in some parts in the summer months. Fortunately, there remain many untouched areas, particularly to the north of the Tarentaise, along the Franco-Italian frontier and within the Vanoise National Park. The inhabitants of the Tarentaise are, in fact, beginning to realise the importance to them of the summer tourist trade and one hears from time to time the phrase "green gold", indicating that the summer visitor has become a client as valued as those who arrive in the winter.

ACCESS AND ACCOMMODATION

Access is straightforward from the UK, especially now the Channel Tunnel is open. Trains, some TGV (high speed), serve Moûtiers and the terminus at Bourg St Maurice. You have to change at Paris and possibly Lyon and Chambéry. The trains are met by buses, or taxis can be hired. Air flights to Geneva or Lyon (Satolas) are quick but require onward transport to the valleys which can be by train or, in the case of Geneva, coach. Cars can be hired by prior arrangement and having such transport allows the starting points of the walks to be reached easily. Indeed, for this reason, it may well be preferable to drive out and have your own transport to hand. The distance from Calais is close to 600 miles (960 kilometres) but can be covered predominantly on motorway and so is possible in one day - preferably with more than one driver. On the other hand, there are many delightful places to visit on the way and the journey can with profit be extended to two or more days.

The fastest route using the maximum of motorway is Calais-Reims on the A26/E17. The motorway effectively continues through Reims, where it is toll-free, then becomes the A4 making for Châlons sur Marne. Prior to Châlons, a new motorway branches off to Troyes, which is followed past Chaumont, Dijon (whereabouts it becomes the A6) and towards Mâcon. Just north of Mâcon take the A40 past Bourg en Bresse as far as Ambérieu en Bugey. Leave the motorway here and go via Lagnieu and Morestel to pick up the A43 to Chambéry, preferably at Chimilin. Leave the motorway at Chambéry and follow signposts to Grenoble/Turin on a bypass through tunnels. The road becomes motorway again and now you make for Albertville. The motorway ends here but an expressway continues as far as Moûtiers. A pleasant deviation, which breaks the tedium of motorway driving and passes through a region well supplied with hotels and restaurants, is to leave the motorway at Troyes and take the N19 to Vendeuvre, then go south to Bar sur Seine on the D443. Follow the N71 past Châtillon sur Seine then take the D32 etc. through Aignay le Duc, Molloy and Is-sur-Tille, bypass Dijon on the east and join the motorway route just south of Dijon.

Many of these roads will be busy on certain weekends in July and August when the French depart or return en masse to or from the holiday regions. It is worth avoiding weekend travel if at all possible, and if not, check with the French Tourist Office which are the busy weekends. Fortunately, the northern part of the route is not on any of the busy axes leading from Paris and so will always be relatively quiet. The A6 can be quite an experience, though. A date to beware is the 15th of August which is the Feast of the Assumption and a national holiday. The roads will be particularly busy and accommodation difficult to find on spec.

Accommodation is available in hotels, in self-catering apartments, which are sometimes called gîtes, or there are many campsites. Details can be obtained from the Office de Tourisme at your chosen base. There is much accommodation available at the ski resorts, which have the advantage of being above the valley and therefore cooler and quieter, but have the disadvantage that if you wish to venture away from the local hills you have to descend to the valley first. In July and August it is, of course, essential to reserve accommodation beforehand, though the previous spring is quite soon enough to do this. Lists of accommodation can also be obtained in the UK but these are not as comprehensive as those available locally.

A list of tourists offices, their addresses and telephone numbers is given below. Note that camping in the wild is only permitted with the permission of the landowner and is prohibited in the Vanoise National Park.

CENTRES, TOURIST OFFICES AND CAMPSITES

The following abbreviations are used in this list:

OT Office de Tourisme; **SI** Syndicat d'Initiative; **SKI** ski resort at high altitude; **C** campsite nearby, followed by its telephone number and its location if not at the same place as the Centre. Two Auberges de Jeunesse are also given. See note on revised telephone numbers under Using the Telephone in France.

AIME	**SI** Avenue Tarentaise, 73210 Aime (79 09 79 79). **C** (79 09 77 61) at Villette.
LES ARCS	**OT** Les Arcs, 73700 Bourg St Maurice (79 07 70 70). **SKI**.
BEAUFORT	**OT** Arêches-Beaufort, 73270 Beaufort (79 38 37 57). **C** (79 38 33 88) near Beaufort and (79 38 12 07) near Lac St Guérin.
BOURG ST MAURICE	**OT** Place de la Gare, 73700 Bourg St Maurice (79 07 04 92). **C** (79 07 03 45).
BOZEL	**SI** Immeuble Bonrieu, 73350 Bozel (79 55 03 77). **C** (79 22 04 80).
BRIDES LES BAINS	**OT** Place Centenaire, 73570 Brides les Bains (79 55 20 64) **C** (79 55 22 74).
CHAMPAGNY	**OT** Résidence du Centre, 73350 Champagny en Vanoise (79 55 06 55). **C** (79 55 03 41) at Champagny le Haut.
COURCHEVEL	**OT** Immeuble la Croisette, 73120 Courchevel 1850 (79 08 00 29). **SKI**.
MÉRIBEL	**OT** Route Plateau, 73550 Méribel les Allues (79 08 60 01). **SKI**.
PEISEY NANCROIX	**OT** Immeuble les Clarines, 73210 Peisey Nancroix (79 07 94 28). **C** at three sites (79 07 91 60), (79 07 92 65) and (79 07 93 07).
LA PLAGNE	**OT** Plagne Centre, 73210 La Plagne (79 09 02 01). **SKI**.
PRALOGNAN	**OT** Avenue de Chasseforêt, 73710 Pralognan la Vanoise (79 08 71 68). **C** (79 08 71 54), (79 08 75 24).
LA ROSIÈRE	**OT** 73700 La Rosière de Montvalezan (79 06 80 51). **SKI**. **C** (79 06 86 21).
SAINTE FOY	**SI** 73640 Ste Foy Tarentaise (79 06 91 70).

SÉEZ **SI** 73700 Séez (79 41 00 15). **C** (79 41 01 05). Auberge de Jeunesse near Longefoy (79 41 01 93).

TIGNES **OT** Immeuble Palafour, 73320 Tignes le Lac (79 06 35 60). **SKI. C** (79 06 41 27) at les Brevières. Auberge de Jeunesse at les Boisses (79 06 35 07).

VAL D'ISÈRE **OT** Immeuble Thovex, 73150 Val d'Isère (79 06 06 60). **SKI. C** (79 06 26 60).

MAP 2. The general areas of Savoie covered in each chapter. The location of the centres mentioned in the introduction is also shown

WHEN TO GO

The alpine walking season traditionally is said to extend from mid June to mid September. The reason behind this is that before and after these dates, the previous winter's snow may remain frozen all day, especially at the higher altitudes, and so be dangerous to cross without the aid of appropriate equipment such as ice axe and crampons. This view does not, however, take account of an asymmetry of the seasons; there will be much less snow left on the ground in September than will be encountered in June.

Snow is much less likely to be an obstacle in the early autumn and, in practice, hillwalking can be continued well into October. For this reason, among others, many of the French writers who describe walks in this region go as far as to recommend the autumn season. In addition, it is cooler late (and early) in the season and accommodation is less difficult to find. On the other hand, bad periods of weather are more likely, with significant snowfall at high altitude, and most refuges are closed by the end of September. Walks of a single day's duration will, nevertheless, be very rewarding in the autumn.

At the same time, it must be emphasised that to the Briton, one of the special features of the Alps is the alpine flower display, which is particularly splendid in the Tarentaise, and many people would be disappointed to miss this colour. The display is best in July and August and, with a few late exceptions, the flowers are fading fast by early September so autumnal visitors will miss them. The Alps are also very green in summer but by mid September the vegetation starts to die back in anticipation of the rigours of winter, and the slopes turn brown to take on an appearance more akin to that of the British hills. The slopes are enlivened by the bilberry wire, which here goes a deep pillar box red, and if the end of season frosts are early the deciduous trees will turn colour to give magnificent autumn displays. Choose, then, July through to October depending upon your priorities and the flexibility of your holidays.

THE WEATHER

The weather in all mountain areas is less reliable than on the surrounding plains, and the Alps are no exception to this rule, though the weather is generally better than on British hills and particularly in the July-August holiday period. Generalising, one can say that May and June in the Alps are mixed, though June can be very pleasant. July and August are sunny and hot with short periods of rain, while September and October are cooler but often fine. The weather in July and August is, however, different in many ways from that of a good British summer. It tends to fall into one of two patterns which may succeed one another. Long periods of up to perhaps ten days of brilliant, often cloudless skies followed by about three days of rainy weather is one sequence that may be experienced, though the periods of fine weather will be shorter in a poor summer. The sunny days will be hot in the valleys but, since the temperature falls significantly with increasing altitude, it will feel much pleasanter above 2000m. The alternative weather pattern is one of a long series of similar days on which the mornings are brilliantly clear but cloud builds up during the course of the day until some time after 4pm. when thunderstorms break out on and around the summits. The clouds disappear overnight. The storms, which the French call *orages,* can be very violent and it is as well not to be caught in one, certainly not on a ridge. Such days are, nevertheless, good for walking, provided the day is arranged so that return to the valley or refuge is made before the storms break out.

It is unadvisable to venture high during bad weather as it can be very cold at altitude. It is also unnecessary, in view of the likelihood of a quick return of good weather.

Winds are not usually a problem and the sort of gale that requires the walker to lean into it seems rare. Indeed, the clouds often appear out of thin air rather than being carried on a wind. On two occasions the writer has experienced sudden bad weather which appeared out of a clear, blue sky that darkened for about half an hour and then the heavens opened to produce, in one case, sluicing rain that drenched us, though less than a mile away left the ground bone dry. The second occasion was equally local but produced half-inch hailstones which really hurt. In both cases, the clouds cleared as rapidly as they had gathered.

Weather forecasts for the region are remarkably accurate and are displayed by most tourist offices. Their precision is such that most of the chance element has been taken out of making any decision as to whether to set out next day or not. In addition, a departmental forecast can be obtained on the telephone which will forecast up to five days in advance, though with decreasing precision, of course. If you can cope with the French language this service is well worth using, though it has become so complicated an operation that I will give a detailed explanation of how to go about it at the end of the introduction.

It is worth making a few further comments on the idiosyncrasies of the weather lore here. The danger of *orages* has already been mentioned. Another word that may well be encountered is *la canicule* or *temps caniculaire* (canicular weather). This is a period of extreme heat which, if it occurs, does so when Sirius (the dog star or canicula in sixteenth-century Italy) rises and sets with the sun between the 22nd of July and the 22nd of August. The term is applied to any hot spell in the summer. The 15th of August is also a useful date to remember. The weather in this part of the Alps is always changeable around this date, though it may not actually rain. Further south it is said invariably to rain on this date, and always has done so when I was there. For many people this is the end of the real summer. Finally, there is the foehn wind to consider. This blows for a few days at a time from autumn through to spring, though it can also appear in summer. It occurs when a wind blows up the boot of Italy, warm and humid from the Mediterranean. When it hits the Alps it rises and cools, clouds form and precipitation occurs, predominantly on the Italian slopes. It hurtles through any gap it can find in the frontier ridge, ie. the cols, warms a little as it descends and the clouds disappear. The result is a hot or relatively hot wind and a bank of cloud whose front hangs stationary over the frontier ridge, even though the wind is trying to sweep it forward into France. During the rare summer foehns, then, it is as well to avoid the Franco-Italian ridge and environs and go instead to the more westerly part of the region, since the wind intensity dies out quickly as you move away from the frontier. The foehn does have the advantage that it often keeps the sky clear over the Tarentaise.

Early September continues apparently as summer to a newly arrived Briton, though it is cooler and less predictable, a tendency which continues into October. In the six autumns that have passed since the author came to live here, one has been perfect (1994), four have been very pleasant and one (1992) rather poor. In fact, only one outing was made in that October. Even in the good autumns, there is always the possibility of significant snowfall, which will persist for a while and render walking difficult, even if only for a day or two. Autumn, then, has an element of bad weather risk, though many may find the prospect of cooler weather alluring and September preferable to the high summer months.

MAPS AND BOOKS

Three different series of maps are available for the region, two French and one Italian. All can be bought in the UK without difficulty and are:

1) **Didier and Richard** (D&R) series at a scale of 1:50,000. No.11, *Massif et Parc National de la Vanoise*, covers almost the whole area, including the Italian frontier walks. It does not cover the Beaufortain, for which Map No.8, *Massifs du Mt Blanc et Beaufortain,* is needed. These maps are excellent and have selected expeditions marked in blue for walks or red for ski outings, to be undertaken in winter and spring. These coloured markings are not particularly accurately placed on the maps but give an indication of the existence or not of paths. It is also possible to buy, as an accompaniment to each map, a small booklet of the same name as the map, and by the same publisher, which gives descriptions in French of the walks marked in colour on the maps.

2) **IGN** (Institut Géographique National) TOP25 series at a scale of 1:25,000. These appear to have replaced the earlier *carte touristique* which covered the region in three maps. Again, selected expeditions are marked in colour though walks are red and ski outings blue, the exact inverse of the D&R convention. The paths are marked with precision on the IGN maps, though I have found the odd case where the map does not seem to agree with what is found on the ground. These maps cover smaller areas than the D&R maps so it is necessary to buy more of them. I prefer them because I find them easier to read, though the information depicted on the two series of maps is very similar. The IGN maps cover the fringes of Italy only.

3) **IGC** (Istituto Geografico Centrale) also publishes a series at a scale of 1:25,000 and covers the Italian side of the frontier ridge. The

Valgrisanche is covered by Map No.102 in this series.

Unfortunately for us, these new series of large-scale maps have produced a serious hiatus in that none covers the Lagi di Bellacomba and surrounding area that are traversed in two of the walks described in Chapter 5. In this case only D&R No.8 is of use. The maps required will be given as necessary in each chapter, TOP25 number first.

Since many people will wish to plan their holiday ahead, they will need to have the maps to hand before they arrive in France. Your local hillsports shop should be able to order them for you, or they can be obtained from:

Stanfords Ltd, 12 Long Acre, London WC2, and The Map Shop, 15 High Street, Upton-on-Severn, Worcs WR8 OHJ (IGN agents).

Another source of maps and walking information are the tourist offices at the various centres. Bourg St Maurice has a map and a booklet available for tourists, Val d'Isère a descriptive leaflet, and so on. It is certainly worthwhile visiting the nearest office to see what sort of information it has, not only for walking but for the many summer activities that each centre arranges for visitors.

The names of places marked on the maps have a number of peculiarities that it is interesting to recognise. The first is that the spelling of names is not consistent from map to map, nor between maps and other modern French literature. It is not clear why this should be, though the fact that this is a frontier region and only recently became part of France (in 1860) may provide some explanation. One of the reasons does appear to be the silent 'x' and 'z'. Thus we see on the TOP25 Map No.3532ET used for Chapter 5 the peak called *Pointe de la Foglietta*. Elsewhere we find the spelling *Fogliettaz*. The pronunciation is the same and the silent ending is peculiar to Savoie. A well known example of this is the name *Chamonix* which is pronounced *Chamouni*, this latter spelling being that used by De Saussure in his book *Premiers Voyages au Mont-Blanc*. The French themselves seem not to be aware of this and strangers to the area may well pronounce the 'x', whereas a local will not. This does make it rather confusing for the outsider!

Spelling of names also may depend upon which side of the Franco-Italian frontier has done the christening. Some places on the frontier ridge may even have two names. For example, the Col du Rocher Blanc and Col Vaudet are one and the same but named, *in*

French, after features on different sides of the ridge. Language differences are more obvious, as in the national names, though even here confusion creeps in, as with Testa del Rutor and Tête du Ruitor, but why Tête du Rutor as on some of the maps? The existence of different names for a unique feature is always a little surprising in view of the fact that French was, and is, spoken on both sides of the frontier. The reason, presumably, is that until quite recently, mountain people did not move very far from their village of origin and saw no need to have the same names in such places. This static existence also results in place names being repeated throughout the region, indeed throughout the Alps. This causes no problems to anyone brought up in a particular community but can be confusing to the outsider. Thus, in the area of the TOP25 map mentioned above, the description Rouge is applied to three different peaks and Rousse to two. Lacs Noir and lacs Blanc abound. There are three places called La Thuile around Bourg St Maurice, in Italy, near Ste Foy and near Vulmix. There are two La Rosières also, and these are distinguished as La Rosière de Bourg and La Rosière de Montvalezan. It is thus imperative to indicate which place is intended when dealing with the area as a whole, and I trust that I will be clear in what follows.

A final point to mention is those pairs of villages with the same name and situated close together and differentiated by the description *Dessus* and *Dessous* (upper and lower). Not a great deal of difficulty here, except that when spoken by a local, these two words are, to my ears at least, almost indistinguishable.

There are several French language walking guides that cover some of the material to be found here. They tend to describe walks making the ascent and descent by the same route, with few circuits, and none deals with the area in a complete way, aiming rather to give a few walks in several widely spaced areas. They are thus invaluable sources of information for anyone wishing to travel further afield or to try something more difficult than I will describe, since certain of them include a proportion of mountaineering expeditions. A few are listed below, in order of publication, and one English work is included which describes a long-distance footpath that traverses Tarentaise and Vanoise.

C. Maly, *Le Massif de la Vanoise*, Denoel, Paris (1976).

S. Coupe and J.P. Martinot, *Lacs de Savoie,* Jacques Glénat, Grenoble (1982).

M. Collins, *Walking in the French Alps: G.R.5,* Cicerone Press, Milnthorpe (1984)

P. Maes, *40 Randonnées en Vanoise,* l'Astrolabe, Paris (1985).

Association de la Grande Traversée des Alps Cimes, *Balades et Randonnées en Beaufortain,* Glénat, Grenoble (1987).

E. Provost, *Sommets pour Tous,* Mercier, Annecy (4th edition, 1990).

Fédération Française de la Randonnée Pedestre, *Tour de la Beaufortain,* ref. 009, Didier & Richard, Grenoble (1990).

B. Brunet, *Randonnées entre Vanoise et Mont-Blanc,* l'Edelweiss, Bourg St Maurice (1993).

ACCOMPAGNATEURS

Most people are aware that in the alpine regions there exist companies of guides who take clients up the mountains by routes that involve glacier and/or rock work. Such people are professionals and have received comprehensive training. In recent years, in response to the demand of walkers, a second professional group has been created, that of the *accompagnateurs,* who take clients for walks below the high mountain regions. They are again trained professionals and may be aspiring guides or may wish to remain as *accompagnateurs.* The *accompagnateurs* have a varied repertoire of walks to suite all ranges of ability. Many of the outings attain altitudes in excess of 3000m and can be quite demanding. All centres have resident *accompagnateurs* (and guides) and publish a programme of walks. The charge is currently 100FF per person per day. Some longer expeditions are also organised involving nights in refuges. For a newcomer to the area, an outing with an *accompagnateur* can be a very useful introduction to walking in the Alps and is to be recommended.

FOOTPATHS

As recently as 1980 many of the footpaths were not well trodden and have only become more worn as walking has developed in the region, a process which has been accelerated by the *accompagnateurs* who have created and are creating new walks. The footpath system is thus still evolving so that some of the descriptions given below may well become somewhat out of date in future years. The maps of the region carry many black lines which signify paths, only some of which have been emphasised by a coloured line to indicate that it is a recommended itinerary. These latter will be, reliably, well marked paths. The black lines mark old paths used by farmers in the hill pastures. They may signify a path which has been made into a "jeepable" track, on the one hand, or alternatively a path that has fallen into disuse or been cut by a landslide.

There are also many tracks that are not marked at all. Most are herdsmen's paths but some are of use to the walker. In addition, there are a number of what is called an *ancien canal d'eau*, which is a ditch cut into the hillside to convey water to the villages before the invention of piped water supplies and black plastic tubing. The outer banking of these ditches provides a useful pathway on some of our walks. The less well marked paths also have a habit of disappearing and reappearing, which can be tiresome when you are not sure of the way. There are probably two reasons for this. Where there is snow cover for a significant part of the summer season, a path will not form, and where the going is very easy, walkers seem to spread out over the ground and only concentrate on a definite line when the terrain become more difficult again and there is really no choice of route. It is, of course, very pleasant to walk where the paths are relatively little used, and there is a marked contrast with the Chamonix Valley, where it is claimed that on a good day there may be 12,000 people on the paths. It follows, however, that walking in the Tarentaise demands an ability to use a map and compass.

In this guide, I use the word "path" to denote a footpath not wide enough or not well enough made to admit the passage of four-wheeled vehicles. You may still encounter scramble motor bikes on such paths as these are used by the farmers to get to the high pastures. Mountain bikes may also pass by, though these are now banned from certain paths. The word "track" is used to denote an unsurfaced road wide enough to take four-wheeled vehicles. A surfaced road is called a road. The state of the paths is generally good and the ground normally stony and reasonably dry under foot. The terrain drains well after rain and it is unusual to encounter the linear morass that sometimes passes for a path in the UK, though there are just one or two places with muddy sections. One type of terrain we do not have in any significant amount in the UK is alder scrub. This occurs above the forest line and is essentially impenetrable. Look for a path through if you are confronted by this obstacle. Interestingly, this scrub was more extensive some centuries ago, but has been progressively cleared by the farmers as they enlarged the mountain pastures. The alpine landscape is thus not as "natural" as it looks. One real danger, if farming is much reduced in the hills, is that this scrub may start to recolonise the slopes with consequent loss of flora.

One problem that has arisen as I have been writing is the question of what to do about signposts. These have been sprouting up all over the place in the last few years at a rate which is impossible to keep up with. I have therefore decided to ignore them in my descriptions so as not to cause confusion. They will, of course, offer you supplementary information.

In addition to signposting, paths on the continent are usually waymarked with blobs of coloured paint, which the French refer to as *balisage*. This is quite useful, though if ever you lose the path, you lose the waymarks as well. If the line of a path has been changed, for instance if a new bridge has been built since I did a walk, the waymarks can be particularly useful to you. Otherwise, if the marks are present, use them as confirmation that you are not the first to have used this particular path, but use the map if they disappear. The system used in Italy is somewhat more elaborate and the waymarks are less easy to lose. However, if in the forest in France, beware foresters' markings which can be confused with waymarking.

You will find that the paths across the high pastures are often cut by orange string, which is an electric fence put there temporarily to control the grazing. It is usually easiest to pass under, though on some much used paths the herdsman may provide a "gate". The fences will generally be energised and the observant may notice a few which are operated by solar electric generators.

All walkers will be familiar with the term *col*, which is a pass where a ridge is crossed at its lowest point. The word *cormet* will also be encountered and has the same meaning as col. The word *passage*, on the other hand, indicates a crossing point on a ridge, but not at a lowest point. It has been suggested to me that these *passages* had something to do with smuggling.

Névé is the name given to the remains of last winter's snow and differentiates the walking in the Alps, perhaps more than anything else, from that in the UK. It forms an extensive cover early in the season but melts rapidly each day as the season progresses and may be almost completely absent by the end of August. Its state depends upon many factors such as the extent of the snowfall the previous winter, the warmth of the spring and the heat of the summer. *Névé* is solid and compacted but has not suffered the transformation to ice that occurs in the glaciers. Its surface becomes rippled, rather like a sea-washed beach, and the ripples provide good foothold. When the surface is frozen, as it may be early in the morning, even in high summer, *névé* is dangerous since a slip can lead to an unstoppable fall. Under such conditions it is necessary to use an ice axe and/or crampons to cross the snow. As the day warms up, the surface of the *névé* will soften and it is then practicable to cross. Special equipment is not necessary, though many walkers are to be observed using ski poles as an aid. Good, rigid boots are, however, essential on snow as the trainer type of footwear is more prone to slipping.

Apart from the obvious danger of a slip and slide, the main danger associated with *névé* is the way it can conceal streams and lakes. The thickness and strength of the snow may be sufficient to hold the weight of a walker early in the season but as the snow melts this assurance becomes less and less reliable. It is therefore imperative **not** to cross *névé* following the bottom of a valley or hollow; always keep up above the lowest part of the slope. The map should also be consulted to see if any lakes are marked as existing under the snow to be crossed, and these should be avoided. At the same time, remember that not all small lakes are marked and that the maps are not infallible. In addition, be careful at the edge of *névé* or around big rocks showing through the snow as this often melts away from the snow-ground interface and will collapse under your feet, resulting in an unpleasant jolt and wet socks.

Note that if *névé* has melted to expose ice, do not try to cross without the correct equipment.

GRADING OF WALKS AND TIME REQUIRED

This is a subject fraught with difficulties since it is almost impossible to be completely objective. The walks are given one of four grades:

Grade 1   A simple walk on good paths with not too much ascent. Within the capabilities of most people.

Grade 2   A longer but still straightforward expedition.

Grade 3   A walk to high altitude which demands a high degree of fitness. The footpath may not always be well marked.

Grade 4   Walks over difficult terrain and/or in exposed positions. Such walks should be avoided by persons who feel unhappy on Striding Edge or Crib Goch.

It cannot be emphasised too much that an individual's reaction to the difficulty of a particular walk depends not only upon the actual difficulties encountered but upon the state of fitness, range of experience, state of fatigue, and so on, of the person concerned. These grades are simply indicative of what the author regards as the relative difficulties of the walks and does not exonerate the individual from exercising proper judgement on a particular walk, whatever its given grade, as to whether it is safe to continue given the current snow and weather conditions and degree of fatigue of members of the party.

Timing a walk is less contentious since you simply have to apply a suitable formula to the distance/height-gain mixture to obtain a figure that is incontestable. The formula will, however, not necessarily apply to a given party and I will explain in detail how I have arrived at the times given for each walk so that parties can make adjustments as necessary for their range of ability. Because most of the walks described cover quite steep terrain, the most influential factor affecting time is the altitude gained on the ascent and the loss on descent. In many cases it is sufficient simply to work out the altitudes of departure and arrival and ignore the horizontal distance covered. The formulae I shall apply are given below with height gain in metres and times in hours.

1.   A day-long walk with little truly horizontal ground
      Time needed = height gain + 300.

2.   A day-long walk with substantial horizontal parts
      Time needed = (height gain + 300) + (horizontal distance in km + 6).

3.   A circuit using refuges, where it is assumed that a heavier load will be being carried in the rucksack
      Time needed = height gain + 250.

4.   Descent will be estimated on circuits as being at the rate of 500m per hour. No time for the descent will be given on walks where the ascent and descent follow the same route.

These times are no more than indications of how long a walk may take. Some parties will be faster, some slower and performance will in any case improve as the holiday proceeds. It is also important to note that **no** allowance has been made for stops to look at the view, eat, etc. Parties should allow appropriate extra time for this.

WALKING STRATEGY

Such a subject may seem superfluous to an experienced walker, but the Alps do have peculiarities not met in the UK. This was emphasised for me on reading a comment written by an English party staying at a friend's apartment in the Tarentaise: "Too hot for serious walking". Well yes, it was a very hot July, in the valley. Above 2000m altitude, on the other hand, the temperature was much more reasonable. And therein lies the secret of pleasurable walking in the Alps in summer: the early start. Ideally, for any long walk to be undertaken in July or August one should aim to set out before 7am. (French time, currently two hours ahead of GMT) and drive to the starting point for the walk. In this way, the walker sets out in the cool of the morning and the major part of the ascent is accomplished before the heat of the day. Overheating on the descent is unlikely and return to base is made early enough to avoid the afternoon thunderstorms, if such are forecast. The heat of the valley often seems incredible after the coolness of the slopes.

One very important effect of the heat, combined with the altitude and predominance of steep ascent, is rapid dehydration. It is thus essential to carry water in one form or another, and I suggest a minimum of 1 litre per person. Many carry the $1^{1}/_{2}$-litre plastic bottles of mineral water available in the shops. It is possible to top up the water at springs, though it is advisable to take care in the choice of such sources. Many streams act as the recipients for the foul water from high-altitude chalets and the pollution is increased by the herds which graze on the alps. Nor should water from glacier streams be used as this may contain powdered rock in suspension and is said to give digestive problems. Food should also be carried, though what and how much will depend upon the individual choice. It is, perhaps, useful to know that French chocolate seems to melt less easily than that bought in the UK. Also most refuges with a guardian will provide food and drink to day visitors at not unreasonable prices.

A second essential for the fair-skinned Briton is some protection from sunburn. There does seem to be a real difference in this respect between ourselves and the locals, who quite suddenly go deep brown about the middle of May and stay that way all summer, whereas I have to be careful not to turn bright salmon pink on the way to tanning. The sun in the clear air of the mountains is very intense and, in any case, contains more UV light than at sea level. The UV content is indeed increasing, perhaps because of ozone layer depletion, and the observatory at the Jungfrau Joch in Switzerland has measured a 10 percent increase in intensity over the last decade. A good sunburn cream should thus be applied to all exposed skin and renewed as necessary. I find the waterproof creams to be best since they resist being washed off by perspiration. Sunglasses will also be useful, especially if you expect to spend time on or near snow, where the reflected light can be very intense.

It should go without saying that any visitor to the Alps should be fit upon arrival, the best way of ensuring this being to undertake some walks before leaving the UK. Even then it is wise to take account of the effects of heat and altitude on performance and work up to the more arduous expeditions. The clothing needed is similar to that which is suitable for walking in the UK. Certainly, take something warm and windproof in case the party is surprised by bad weather. This is important since the drop in temperature which occurs with an adverse change in the weather is much more marked than is usual in the UK. At the same time expect it to be hot, particularly on the ascent, and wear light clothing with the rest in reserve in the rucksack. Shorts are ideal in high summer, some even use bathing suits, but warm clothing must be carried. (I once passed two young women on the way from Pont St Charles to the Prariond refuge who were clad in nothing but bikinis and boots. Half an hour later the afternoon thunderstorms broke! I often wonder how they fared - perhaps there were boyfriends somewhere with big rucksacks.) As far as footwear is concerned, some of the walks will provide no difficulties to people wearing trainers, but I would advise that some form of boot be worn, with cleated sole, capable of coping with rough or wet ground and giving some support for the ankle.

It is assumed, in writing each of the chapters, that the party has its own transport. This means that you can stay at a centre in the valley and drive to the starting point for each walk, a strategy which means that no use need be made of refuges, which are often crowded at the height of the summer. A party without transport has several options. They can hire a taxi for the ascent, though this is not cheap. If they arrange to go out with an *accompagnateur* there may be sufficient transport available within the group to accommodate a few car-less walkers. They may wish to camp above the valley at a centre suitable for several walks but it would be wise in such a case to ask at the local tourist office if camping is acceptable at the chosen spot and whom to ask for permission. Perhaps the best solution, however, is to string a sequence of walks together in a way which allows you to remain high and stay in a refuge or refuges for several nights, descending to the valley to recuperate. With this in mind, I have arranged that the sketch maps relate the walks to one another and indicate all the refuges in the terrain covered by each. I also give a summary of refuges later in this introduction.

One question to be settled by any party is whether to set out in poor weather. If bad weather occurs during a tour there may not be much choice, unless the weather is so bad that you are inevitably stuck in the refuge. In the case of a day outing, however, it is probably best not to go out if the day is poor. The weather is generally so good that it is not really necessary to take the risk involved, since there is virtually bound to be an improvement quite soon. It is also a shame to miss the scenic value of the Alps. Remember that the adage "rain before seven, fine before eleven" has no relevance here as it is unusual for a poor morning to clear quickly.

A final point worth mentioning is that of foot care. Most people will be likely to take the materials they know to be effective for themselves, but in case it is necessary to buy locally there are one or two points that it is useful to know. First, the brand name Elastoplast is not known in France. A similar range of dressings is sold under a variety of proprietary names but, to avoid confusion, it would be wise to show the pharmacist a sample of what is required. To add to the confusion it is possible to buy Elastoplaste - note the 'e' at the end - which is a linen type of bandage with one face covered with adhesive and a protective cover over that. It is sold in various widths and is very effective in protecting known vulnerable points on the foot, prior to the formation of blisters. If blisters do form, Compeed patches are very effective. They are thick in the centre and thin at the edges and so protect the blister, and also have an active healing effect.

SECURITY

Walkers do, unfortunately, have accidents in this region. Many of the causes will be familiar to the UK reader: fatigue, getting benighted, losing the way, all can lead to the need for assistance. Falling on *névé* is an event not encountered in the UK, an event which can be particularly grave in its consequences if the victim encounters rocks on the way down. The possibility of falling through snow bridges has already been discussed; the risk is minimised by avoiding snow-filled hollows and the bottoms of snow-filled valleys or gullies. One quite significant risk is that of slipping and falling on steep grassy slopes which have become wet due to rainfall. Many of the really mild-looking grassy slopes are in fact both long and very steep, much steeper than is usual in the UK. Purchase for the foot is very meagre and the temptation to cross such slopes should be avoided if it has been, or is, raining. Scree can be crossed with care. Running scree seems to be rare though a careful lookout should be kept for falling stones, which have a long way to fall and can be extremely dangerous.

Mountain rescue is reached by dialling 79 07 01 10 (Bourg St Maurice) or 79 08 71 15 (Pralognan la Vanoise). Alternatively, dialling 17 obtains the police. (Please see note on revised numbers under Using the Telephone in France.) Note that once set in motion, a rescue attempt has to be paid for and that suitable insurance is necessary. If it is necessary to communicate with a rescue helicopter, the standard signs are both arms raised means "yes, we need help", one arm raised and one pointing down means "we need no help".

Another slight hazard which it is perhaps as well to be aware of is the existence of a significant adder population. The walker seldom seems to see them - I saw none for ten consecutive years and then encountered three during the eleventh season. They mostly keep out of the way and, I suspect, need to be harassed for them to attack. Bilberry pickers sometimes get bitten and they also frequent wild raspberry thickets. It is possible to buy for about £12 an anti-venom serum though I am advised that if not kept cool this can be more dangerous than the bite itself. A much cheaper, and probably safer, alternative is to carry a suction device called Aspivenin, which is sold by pharmacists. If bitten, suck out as much venom as possible, then walk back to the valley for assistance, without hurrying and with a light tourniquet applied high up the bitten limb.

Streams can present problems to the unwary and in two different ways. The first is man-made and arises because of the extensive hydro-electric development of the region. Water is the raw material of this technology and is moved about the mountains in tunnels and by using the existing water courses. It is therefore dangerous to mess about in many of the mountains streams and yellow warning notices are posted where there is this danger. These notices should not be taken lightly since if a sluice somewhere is opened, the water level can rise several feet in a few seconds. Some friends were caught in this way and felt lucky to have got to the safety of the bank in time. The second problem is a natural one. Early in the morning it may be quite easy to cross an unbridged glacier stream, but as the day progresses and the ice starts to melt, the water flow increases markedly so that it may be quite difficult or even impossible to ford in the afternoon. Wading is not advisable since the water is very cold, your boots may fill with fine gravel, and in some cases the flow may be fast enough to sweep along big stones which will cause considerable personal damage.

It goes without saying that if you encounter anyone else in difficulties you should give all the assistance that is within your power, even though language difficulties may be a hindrance. Apart from any moral obligation to fellow walkers it is of interest to know that under French law it is an offence not to help someone in danger.

REFUGES

There are many mountain refuges within the area. These provide simple bunkhouse accommodation, though the standard is gradually being improved. Some are without guardian, in which case cooking facilities are provided and all provisions have to be carried by the user. There is no control over the numbers using the refuge and it may be very crowded and noisy. It is essential to arrive early if walking in the high season. The majority of the refuges, do however, have a guardian and provide both self-catering and demi-pension accommodation - dinner, bed and breakfast, costing about 140FF per person. In order to reduce the overcrowding of these refuges, most of them are now connected to the telephone service and it has become essential, in some cases obligatory, to reserve places in advance, a few days' notice being necessary for the most popular refuges. Where a refuge is mentioned in the text, its details will be given at the end of the section. A summary of all these refuges is given below, together with details of some additional ones, and the location is shown on the map. Refuges are indicated by a black square on the maps given in each chapter.

Further details of these and other refuges can be found in a booklet, No 1. of *Les Guides de la Grande Traversée des Alps* available in local bookshops. Refuges are operated by several organisations such as the Club Alpin Français (CAF), or the Vanoise National Park (PNV), or they may belong to the local commune or be run privately. Refuges with a guardian are open from about mid June to mid or end September, though the times vary from year to year, so check if walking late in the season. Some such refuges provide shelter outside these dates, often only a part of the accommodation remaining open. Some refuges without a guardian may be permanently open, others require a key to be collected from the valley.

Refuges on the Italian side of the frontier are more expensive than the French (about 200FF per person) and will take payment in French francs. French is spoken commonly, but not necessarily English.

Finally, it is useful to take a sheet sleeping bag and a torch to refuges. You can, of course, take a down bag but this is not really necessary at the low altitude refuges mentioned here.

The Lauzière in late autumn, Grand Pic to the left.
On the way up to Les Arangles, Mt Blanc in the distance and the hills of
Beaufortain in the middle distance.

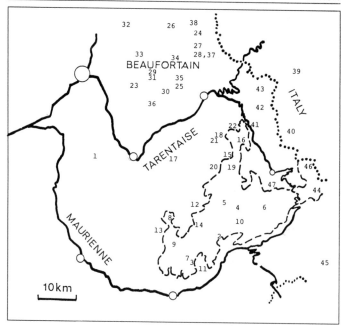

MAP 3. The approximate location of the refuges mentioned in the introduction and following chapters

Summary of refuges

Chapter 1 - La Lauzière

1.   Des Fées, alt. 1850m, no guardian, 26 beds (79 24 08 98).
     Telephone five days in advance to book and organise collection
     of key. Situated above Celliers.

Chapter 2 - Around Pralognan

2.   Arpont, Walk 3.
3.   Dent Parrachée, Walk 3.
4.   Entre Deux Eaux, Walk 3.

*The Glacier des Grandes Couloirs leads to the summit of the Grande Casse. View
from near the Col de la Vanoise*

5. Felix Faure or Col de la Vanoise, Walk 3.
6. Femma, alt. 2370m, meals provided, 48 beds (79 20 50 85). Closes early September. PNV, situated in Vallon de la Rocheure, east of Entre Deux Eaux. Radio link via Plan du Lac refuge.
7. Fond d'Aussois, Walk 3.
8. Lacs Merlet, alt. 2417m, no guardian, 14 beds. PNV, situated south of Courchevel.
9. Péclet-Polset, Walk 5.
10. Plan du Lac, alt. 2364m, meals provided, 64 beds (79 20 50 85). Closes end September. PNV, situated south of Entre Deux Eaux.
11. Plan Sec, alt. 2350m, meals provided, 80 beds (79 20 31 31). Closes mid September. Private, situated south-east of Fond d'Aussois.
12. Pralognan, alt. 1418m. Three gîtes (79 08 72 59), (79 08 72 73), (79 08 73 11)) (guardian 79 08 74 14). There is also a refuge, Le Repoju, whose guardian can be contacted on 79 08 73 79.
13. Saut, Walk 5.
14. Valette, Walk 3.

Chapter 3 - Bourg St Maurice to Champagny

15. Entre le Lac, alt. 2145m, meals provided, 45 beds (79 09 52 48) (radio link). Closes early October. Private, situated by the Lac de la Plagne.
16. Martin, Walk 8.
17. Mont Jovet, Walk 1.
18. Mont Pourri, Walk 8.
19. Palet, Col du, alt. 2650m, meals provided, 48 beds (79 07 91 47). Closes mid September. PNV, situated west of Val Claret, Tignes.
20. Plaisance, Walk 3.
21. Rosuel, Walk 3.
22. Turia, Walk 8.

Chapter 4 - Beaufortain and Northern Tarentaise

23. Arolles, Walk 7.
24. Balme, Walk 7. | Two refuges with the same name.
25. Balme, Walk 7. |

26. Bellasta, Walk 7.
27. Bonhomme, Walk 6.
28. Chapieux, alt. 1552m, meals possible, 10 beds. Private.
29. Clarines, Walk 7.
30. Coire, Walk 4.
31. Grangette, Walk 7.
32. Lachat, Walk 7.
33. Pemonts, Walk 7.
34. Plan de la Lai, Walk 6.
35. Presset, Walk 7.
36. Nant du Beurre, Walk 4.
37. Nova, Walk 6.
38. Roselette, Walk 7.

Chapter 5 - Les Chapieux to the Nant Cruet

39. A. Deffeyes, alt. 2494m, meals provided, 70 beds (19 39 16 58 84 23) (Italy). Situated between the Glacier and Cascades du Rutor.
40. Mario Bezzi, Walk 8.
41. Monal, Walk 8.
42. Motte or de l'Archeboc, Walk 8.
43. Ruitor, alt. 2030m, 45 beds. Private. Situated above La Savonne.

Chapter 6 - Around Val d'Isère

44. Carro, alt. 2670m, meals provided, 77 beds (79 05 95 79). CAF. See map of Walk 7.
45. Evettes, alt. 2590m, meals provided, 65 beds (79 05 96 64). CAF. See map of Walk 8.
46. Fond des Fours, alt. 2537m, meals provided, 42 beds (79 06 16 90). PNV. See map of Walk 5.
47. Prariond, alt. 2300m, meals provided, 42 beds (79 06 06 02). PNV. See map of Walk 2.

Note that some refuges without a guardian may be surveyed during July and August and that some refreshments may be available during the day. This enables bookings to be made by would-be users and also ensures that certain "indelicate persons", as the French describe them, have to pay for their night's lodging!

SOME GENERAL INFORMATION

Geology

The geology of the Tarentaise-Vanoise region is very complex and indeed is not yet fully understood. The story starts about 300 millions years ago when the sea separating the continents that were to become Africa and Europe started to widen. Initially there was a region of lakes in which there were marshes and into which erosion deposited sandstone and other debris. These eventually became the present day anthracite measures (which were mined until quite recently) black schist and sandstone, all of the Carboniferous era. Further sandstone deposits were made as the region submerged and then the deposition of chalk formed from the skeletons of living organisms gave an upper layer of limestone 300 to 600m in thickness. At much the same time, the evaporation of a substantial body of sea water produced an evaporite deposit in which gypsum was a particularly important constituent, though there was also salt and no doubt some dolomite. There was then an uplifting and fracturing of these rocks and further deposition in the shallow seas that remained, of mixtures of chalk and sand. As the sea widened there was again submergence of the land, and rocks of the mantle or crust were thrust among the sedimentary strata.

Then, about 50 million years ago, the continents started to drift together and all that had been laid down was compressed eventually into less than one-tenth of its original area. Strata rode over and under one another and were folded, concertina like. The enormous pressures and the high temperatures metamorphosed the rocks into the forms we see today. Gypsum is a single substance and does not metamorphose but is very plastic under these conditions and acted as a lubricant between strata, facilitating the movement. One source suggests that there was a movement of material from the east, which was uplifted first, and essentially slid over the gypsum under the forces of gravity. The plastic gypsum was also injected into faults and so became widely distributed with a significant effect on the morphology of the mountain. The metamorphosis process resulted in sandstone being converted into quartzite, the chalky deposits to limestone or marble and the mixed deposits to a schisty rock containing mica flakes which make it sparkle in the sun. These rocks are known as the lustrous schists and can be very attractive. The rocks of the mantle below the sea were transformed into green serpentine. This uplifting was accompanied by strong erosion and fracturing and several domes of the old underlying crystalline quartzitic micaschists emerged and today form some of the major summits (Mt Pourri, Bellecôte, Dome de Chasseforêt).

The types of rock encountered during a walk are thus likely to be quite varied. Places where some of the rocks mentioned above will be seen are:

Chapter 2, Walk 6 - The Dent du Villard and Petit Mt Blanc de Pralognan are mountains of gypsum. Since this mineral is slightly soluble in water, the gypsum regions are characterised by water erosion and craters (swallow holes or dolines) where water has gone underground. These craters are often a sign that you are in gypsum country. Anyone who has skied at La Plagne, for instance, will no doubt have wondered what has caused the curious deep holes to form in the plateau between La Grande Plagne and Plagne Bellecôte. Close to gypsum deposits, you often find what the French geologists call *cargneules*. This is dolomite which has been eroded under pressure by sulphatic water and looks like tufa, though its mode of formation is different. This rock is full of holes often lined with crystals.

Chapter 2, Walk 5 - Limestone and *cargneules* are found south of Petit Mt Blanc and give some very strange scenery here.

Chapter 3, Walk 1; Chapter 6, Walk 3; Chapter 6, Walks 1, 4 & 6. - Lustrous schists are found in the Nant Cruet and Rocher de la Davie, around the Col de l'Iseran and the Points des Lorès.

Chapter 3, Walk 8 - The tour of Mt Pourri takes you through glacier morain and the denuded base crystalline rocks, though there is a small limestone area near the Col de la Sachette.

Chapter 5, Walk 12 - Serpentine will be seen on the crossing of the Col du Rocher Blanc (Col Vaudet).

A short account such as the above cannot hope to give any real idea of the complexity of the region and those who wish to know more detail should consult a recent French book: J. Debelmas and J.P. Rampnoux, *Guide Géologique du Parc National de la Vanoise*, Éditions BRGM, Orléans, 1994. This book, which is illustrated by colour photographs and line drawings, gives a fuller account of the geology and suggests several "journeys of discovery" to see the features described. There is also a geological map of the Vanoise at a scale of 1:100,000 in a folder in the back which is extremely useful.

Glaciation has, of course, played a major part in shaping the relief of the region. Some tens of thousands of years ago the glaciers extended as far as Chambéry and Grenoble and their thicknesses were great; the altitude of the surface at Grenoble was 1100m (ground level is now 214m) and at Moûtiers 1900m (now 480m). The present summits showed through this ice cover but the glaciers shaped and widened the valleys and sculpted their floors while higher up they formed cirques, sharpened the ridges, and where cirques overlapped, isolated peaks or horns were formed. Erosion has continued since the ice retreated and indeed is still taking place, sometimes quite dramatically when a mud slide cuts the main roads.

The extent of glaciation has been measured systematically since 1870-1880. There has been an overall retreat of the ice during this time, though with peaks of glacier advance at around 1890, 1920 and possibly 1940. We have just passed through a period of advance which terminated somewhere between 1980 and 1990 and the ice seems again to be in retreat. Certainly, there have been significant reductions in ice cover in the Tarentaise region in the last five years.

Flora

The summer show of flowers in the Alps is legendary and embellishes any expedition undertaken between the beginning of July and early September. The Tarentaise region is particularly favoured with an abundant flora and many visitors would like to have some idea of the names of the plants that they see. The lower slopes are full of flower early in the season and the colour climbs as the season advances. Many plants have to wait until the snow melts and it is often possible to observe around a still thick snowdrift a succession of flowers appearing each at a particular distance from its edge, dictated by how long the ground there has been clear of snow; a sort of time capsule, where different stages of the season co-exist simultaneously.

Blue gentians abound, the similar species *verna* and *bavarica* being in evidence most of the season, despite the significance of the

Primula hirsuta

name *verna*, which means spring flowering. The trumpet gentian hereabouts is the species *kochii* and while locally very abundant, has a relatively short flowering period in each locality. There are many other blue flowered species and in addition one purple and two yellow gentians may be seen. One is particularly tall, *gentiane jaune* or *Gentian lutea*, which can be up to 2m high. The roots are used to make an alcoholic drink called *gentiane*. The alpine pansy, *Viola calcarata*, is very common and has typically rich purple flowers with a yellow eye, though there are several colour variations about.

A very striking flower common in the region is the yellow anemone which the French call *anemone soufré* and whose botanic name is *Pulsatilla alpina subspecies apiifolia*. This is a large flower of 5cm diameter or more and of a lovely clear pale yellow. Where it grows, it can occur by the tens of thousands. There is a white form

A large clump of Androsace alpina *on the slopes below the Col de la Galise (Chapter 6)*

Thlaspi rotundifolium *which grows only in scree and has a scent of honey. Called locally the Tabouret (stool) des Alpes*

also, though this is less common in the Tarentaise. Both have striking seed heads. Less common, particularly in summer, when it will only be seen growing in rocks above 2000m altitude, is the pink primrose *Primula hirsuta,* which glows at you from a shady niche. The best time to see this flower is in late May when it forms mats of colour on the cliffs above Le Crot (Chapter 5).

A very common family of flowers which is met at all altitudes is that of the campanulas, with their bells of various colour but usually shades of blue. They tend to flower late in the season and so extend the time during which flowers are in evidence. There are a number of species related to our harebell but mostly you will remember the upright stems and hairy, hanging bells of *Campanula barbata,* in colour varying from white to deep blue, the tall spikes of *C. spicata,* the curious tight yellow pokers of *C. thyrsoides,* the low mats of *C. cochliarifolia* and, more rarely, the blue-grey flowers of *C. cenisia,* growing in rocky moraine where nothing much else can get a foothold, or *C. allionii* with its enormous blue bells competing in size with a garden-grown Canterbury bell. I have only seen this last on the tour of the glacier of the Vanoise.

At higher altitudes the flora is less abundant but still striking. Two white buttercups must be mentioned, *Ranunculus alpestris* and *R. glacialis.* The former bas bright green leaves and flowers which are always white and grows in masses wherever it occurs. *R. glacialis* has much fleshier leaves of a duller green and changes in colour from white to deep pink after fertilisation. This plant seeks out places where there is plenty of moisture. Growing on the highest

*The magnificent though rare
Lys orange or Orange lily*

rocks and scree you may see *Androsace alpina,* varying in colour from white to pink and the small flowers almost completely hiding the tight cushion of tiny leaves. Growing in stony scree you can sometimes see the pale purple *Thlaspi rotundifolia* with its strong scent of honey. The edelweiss grows hereabouts too, though it is a flower whose abundance varies widely from year to year.

I should also mention the family of plants known as the *génépi* which are three species of *artemisia* with grey foliage and not very conspicuous yellow flowers in August. The plants grow at high altitude and the flowers have been coveted for centuries for their medicinal virtues. They can be steeped in alcohol and the resulting highly flavoured liquor either added to hot water to make a herb tea, or sugar is added to make an aperitif. The *génépi* hunters are to be seen in August, outside the National Park (where culling flowers is forbidden), whole families with plastic bags, in unlikely places. Most mountain people prepare *génépi.* It is said to have excellent restorative properties and many other beneficial effects. Once tasted you can detect one of the principal elements of Green Chartreuse.

Two magnificent lilies may also be seen. The orange lily flowers in June on rock ledges and is only found in a few inaccessible places. On the other hand, the Martagon lily is found in small groups all over, including woodland. It is tall and varies in colour from a dull pink to a really striking rose.

This list gives only a slight idea of the richness of the flora. A much better view can be obtained from the many books that have been written on the subject. Two handbooks that are small enough to fit in the rucksack are:

Another widely distributed plant, Silene acaulis. It usually grows in the form of a flattened cushion but this enormous clump was found just below the Col du Mont (Chapter 5).

A. Huxley, *Mountain Flowers*, Blandford Press, Poole (1978).

C. Grey-Wilson, *The Alpine Flowers of Britain and Europe*, William Collins Sons & Co Ltd, London (1979).

These will assist the the walker to identify many species on the spot. Though be warned - it is a time-consuming process which can become a passion. A third book, which is too big and too valuable for the rucksack but which contains beautiful photographs of most of the species of flower found in the Tarentaise, is:

E. Danesch and O. Danesch, *Le Monde Fascinant de la Flore Alpine*, Didier-Richard (1981).

Fauna

The region has a number of indigenous mammals, large and small, many of which are not found in the UK and which may be seen during outings. The largest is the bouquetin, a relative of the Arabian ibex. It has very little fear of man and it was possible for hunters to approach very closely, almost to put a gun in an ear, and kill it easily. As a result, the numbers dwindled and there remained only 40 animals. It was thus decided to create the Vanoise National Park to protect them and extend the sanctuary area already available in the Gran Paradiso National Park, just across the border in Italy. This measure has been spectacularly successful and the numbers have now multiplied many times. They remain easy to approach and it is possible almost to walk among a herd and photograph them. The males have large curving horns. The females are much

Male bouquetin lying

smaller. The sexes graze apart for most of the year but in quite large herds.

Smaller, more attractive but very difficult to approach is the chamois with its short, back curved horns. This may be encountered in herds or as single animals but all quickly move away from the intruder. They cross difficult, rocky ground with incredible grace. I remember a single animal that wished to cross the path of our party and did so in a wide circling movement until able to cross a river in a wall of spray.

The third mountain dweller that is likely to be seen and very much heard is the lovable marmot. It is reminiscent of a beaver in appearance, though the tail is not as big. The colour varies from brown to golden. They live in deep burrows and when disturbed run for cover but often pause at the entrance to the burrow for a good look at the cause of disturbance, standing on their hind legs to get a better view. When a human appears in marmot country, distant animals emit a shrill whistling shriek to warn other marmots. Those near stay wisely quiet, though if they feel safe and out of sight can sometimes be seen peeping above the vegetation to observe what is going on. The best time to see them is in the early morning. In the National Park they have become remarkably tame and can be photographed without too much difficulty. They hibernate from mid October to mid April, in burrows deep in the ground, when their heartbeat rate falls to two to three beats a minute. They awake every five days or so to perform their toilet.

Young marmot outside its burrow

Other wild animals that may be encountered high in the mountains are the ermine or stoat, the weasel, the fox, whose presence causes high vocal activity among marmots, the mountain hare and the mouflon, which is a sheep with spiral horns. At rather lower altitudes live the wild boar. These tend to remain well concealed, though locals have advised us to take a stick with us if we walk in the woods near home in case we meet a frisky one! They are more usually detected by finding dug up sections of mountainside where they have been grubbing for food. We have also seen red deer, badger and red squirrels in the pinewoods, though these last are much larger and darker than those found in the UK.

Many species of bird live in the valleys and there are a few seen constantly high in the mountains. The raven with its hoarse croak and the chough with its sharp whistle echoing off the cliffsides are common. Birds of prey are omnipresent and several of the larger species are represented. The golden eagle breeds here and can be seen soaring high in the hills, while buzzards fly frequently at the lower altitudes. It is also possible to find the bearded vulture, a bird which had become extinct in the Alps but which has been reintroduced over the last twenty years. The kestrel will also be encountered and sometimes can be observed from above as it glides below a ridge. On the ground you may disturb ptarmigan or partridge and there are still black grouse in the pine forests, though these are on the decline due to the development of the ski resorts. The alpine swift is impressive as it skims the ridges, sometimes almost passing between your legs.

Insects are represented principally and visibly by the butterflies and moths. These are attracted to high altitudes by the flowers and are a common sight. We have seen red admirals at 2500m, much higher than our books suggest is their limit. Their caterpillars will also be seen, some very gaudy and large. A common sight is a cloud of small butterflies collected around a wet patch in a path. These are called blues on account of the colour of the male, though the female is a dull brown. Also audibly striking is the noise of grasshoppers, which make an incredible din in the pastures on hot days. Flies are not really a problem, except on the pastures where animals are grazed. Nor is there anything to compete with the Scottish midge.

The Vanoise National Park

The Vanoise National Park was created in 1963 with an area of about 600 square kilometres. The relief, flora and fauna are absolutely protected and hunting and collection of all vegetable material is forbidden. Within the park have been created some 450km of footpaths and a chain of refuges managed by the park, which permits access to the whole of the region. There are, naturally, regulations which the walker is expected to obey and these are posted at all the principal entrances to the park on either road or footpath. To give the regulations teeth, the park wardens are empowered to levy substantial on-the-spot fines for any transgressions. There must be no picking of the flowers, no harassment of the fauna, no rubbish left about, no camping except in emergency, and no dogs even if on a lead. The park authorities are also trying to discourage walkers from cutting the bends on zig-zag paths as it is becoming apparent that this practice is causing erosion. In certain places the short cuts have been blocked off. This seems a very sensible precaution when one remembers the state of some of the hill paths in the UK. The footpaths are well signposted with distances expressed in terms of the time needed to reach the signposted objective.

Outside the park there is a buffer zone called the pre-park, from which the park's development is directed and within which human activity particular to the mountains is encouraged. Many of the ski resorts lie within this region.

The park has a group of technical personnel to deal with the health and development of the wild animals within the park, and initiate visitors into an understanding of flora and fauna and geology by means of outings, which are advertised at tourist offices.

Food and Drink

Like the rest of France, Savoie is very proud of its regional cooking and wines. These are relatively little known in the UK and a few words indicating what you should look for will be useful.

The wines may be white, rosé or red and the majority of those sold are *apellation controllée* or AC. The white wines are quite unique and can be very refreshing drunk cold on a hot day. They are named according to the place where they are produced and the better ones also have the name of the producer on the label. Seyssel has a reputation outside Savoie but is not always available in the shops and can be expensive. Chignian is good. Apremont is noticeably *pétillant* and is the wine traditionally drunk with cheese fondue. Other good named whites are Cruet, Crepi, Abymes and Rousette, though I find the first two to have a rather sharper taste than the others. You can sometimes see white *ordinaires* made from the Jacquère grape and these are also delicious. The AC red wines are named after the grape used in their production - gamay, mondeuse, pinot - and the better quality ones also carry the name of the place of production - Gamay de Chignian or Mondeuse d'Arbin, for example. The gamays can have a remarkable resemblance to Beaujolais. The rosés are also pleasant drinks and, again, differ from the rosés found in other regions. The stronger drinks *Gentiane* and *Génépi* have been mentioned in the section on flora.

The regional food has its roots in the farming traditions of yesteryear. Raw materials are dairy products, potatoes and pork and can be very rich, as if designed to keep out the winter's cold. As a starter one is often offered *jambon cru*, which is raw ham dried in chalets high in the mountains and served in thin slices. *Saucisses de Savoie* are pure pork sausages and appear on menus as *diots au vin blanc*, in which guise they are delicious. Potatoes appear more and more frequently in the restaurants in the form of *gratin savoyard*, in which thin slices are cooked with stock, cheese and garlic in a dish which is very close to *gratin Dauphinois* - not to be confused with *pommes dauphinées*.

Much cheese is produced in the area, the pride being Beaufort. This is made in enormous round moulds and is distinguished by having concave sides. In summer it is made high in the mountains, the milk being collected in mobile milking sheds which are towed into place behind a tractor. In winter it is made in the farms and cooperatives. It is thus sold as *Beaufort d'Été* (or *d'Alpage*) and *Beaufort d'Hiver*, the summer variety having the better flavour. It is a good cheese to take for sustenance on an outing. Other cheeses are *tomme de Savoie*, which is sold in several varieties differing by their fat content and whether they are produced from fresh or pasteurised milk, *tamié* which is made by the monks in the monastery near the col of the same name, and *reblochon* which comes from the range of the Aravis to the north of the Beaufortain. Many small goats' cheeses are also made.

Two regional specialities which you will often see advertised are rich main meals based on cheeses. One is *fondue Savoyarde* which consists of a mixture of cheeses, including some Beaufort, melted with white wine (Apremont), kirsch and garlic. It is served on a small spirit stove to keep it fluid and eaten by dipping chunks of bread in the melt so as to coat them with cheese. The other is *raclette*, in which melted cheese is poured onto chunks of boiled potato and these are eaten with the accompaniment of a selection of cooked meats.

Finally, a tip for those who like their bacon. Do not ask for "bacon" as this is a form of cooked meat. For the purposes of a fry-up, ask for *poitrine fumé en tranche*, which makes an excellent smoked, streaky bacon.

The Off Day

Much of the summer activity in the Tarentaise valleys is devoted to sporting interests but there are many less energetic things to do for those wishing for a pause. Here are some suggestions.

The baroque decorated churches in the valley are quite splendid. The region is strongly Catholic, indeed the Church can be expected to be strong in an environment beset by apparently uncontrollable natural disasters. At the time of the Protestant reformation the Church here responded by engaging in sumptuous redecoration of the interior of the churches in baroque style. Complex and colourful retables were built behind the altars, supported typically by curly columns and adorned by stucco statues. These are well worth seeing and details of opening times can be obtained at tourist offices. There are baroque churches at Hauteville-Gondon, Peisey-Nancroix, Landry, Bellentre, Séez, Vulmix, Montvalezan, Ste Foy, Tignes, Val d'Isère and Champagny. Each summer there is a music festival of recitals by many artists which takes place in these baroque churches, and some of these may be of interest to the visitor.

Two other religious edifices worth visiting are the Basilica at Aime, and Notre Dame des Vernettes. The Basilica is an obvious and imposing building beside the main road through Aime. It is no longer used for worship but is a museum. It is very old, with Roman connections. Notre Dame des Vernettes is reached by turning sharp right above the last shops at Plan Peisey and driving until the first hairpin is reached, at which point it is possible to park. Follow the track, taking the first fork right and continue for some 2km. The church is nestled below the Aiguille Rousse in a very imposing position, which it owes to the presence of a miraculous source on the hillside below. A series of crosses has been erected between church and source and the scene is very impressive on Good Fridays when skiers descend to join in the service of the stations of the cross.

Coming to more modern times, Electricité de France will show visitors around the hydro-electric generating station of le Malgovert, where you can get an idea of the extent of the construction work that has gone into harnessing the "white coal" in this part of the world. The station is situated beside the Les Arcs road, on the river, between Séez and Bourg St Maurice.

The Col du Pt St Bernard is also worth a visit, preferably in reasonable weather. Just before the col there is a garden in which are planted many species of alpine flower. This is la Chanousia, a garden founded in 1897 by the abbé Chanoux. It was abandoned

and destroyed in 1940 and then reconstruction recommenced in
1976. Open every day, there is an entry fee. Further on, at the
summit of the col, on the right looking into Italy, there is a stone
column. This is Jupiter's Column or *Colonne de Joux* and is Roman.
Jupiter once held a torch to guide travellers. Last century the statue
of Jupiter was removed and replaced by one of St Bernard. There is
also a museum devoted to the abbé Chanoux.

There are indeed several local museums throughout the region
and details can be obtained at tourist offices. Some suggestion are
the costume museum at Hauteville-Gondon, which has a display of
the local traditional dress, the Arpin weaving factory between Séez
and Bourg St Maurice, which has examples of the ancient ways of
producing cloth, or the little museum on the Côte d'Aime where the
old country ways are shown as well as the technique used for
producing the local cheeses. Modern cheesemaking can be seen in
the cheese cooperative at Bourg St Maurice and there is a folk
museum and craft shops at Séez, as well as a tannery and a
taxidermist with a small natural history museum. Most places have
an annual summer fête.

The Short Walks

I propose at the end of each chapter a few short walks at lower
altitudes. Some are fragments of the main walks described in the
chapter, while others are quite independent of the rest and cover
new ground. I also suggest some attractive picnic places which
require little effort to find. These outings are all graded 1 or 2 and are
aimed at the less active members of a party or could be used on an
off day. It must be emphasised that the number of low level walks
possible is legion and that those described are simply the ones
known to, and liked by, the author. A glance at the relevant TOP25
map will suggest many other walks to explore in this delightful
countryside.

Using the Telephone in France

It is, of course, much more difficult to converse in a foreign language
on the telephone than it is face to face, and some persistence is
required. If you are lucky, there may be someone at the other end
who can speak English, but this cannot be relied upon and in any

case they have the same difficulties as you on the telephone. Three possibilities I will cover are:

1: Ringing another number in France, such as a refuge or tourist office. With the exception of the Paris region, all numbers comprise eight figures, which the French think of as four two-figure numbers. Thus 79 07 04 92 is verbally seventy-nine, seven, four, ninety-two - but in French, of course! Dialling will produce first a train of rapid pips which indicate that you are being connected, though if the connection is immediate these will not be heard. The ringing tone is a slowly repeated long note, the engaged tone is a faster version of this.

2: Ringing a number in the UK or other country. First dial 19. This will be followed more or less rapidly by a buzzing tone indicating that you are connected to the international exchange. When you hear this tone dial 44 (the national code) and then the UK number preceded by the STD code **less** the first zero. For example, if the UK number is 0154 2367, dial (19-) 44 154 2367. The same applies to calls to Italy except that the national code is 39.

3: Dialling for the French weather forecast is designed for the computer age. Start by dialling 36 68 02 73. You will hear the rapid pips, possibly the ringing tone, then a jingle and an announcement that you are through to Metéo France. You will then get a message which translates as "If you are using a press button telephone then press right away on the starred button, if not then wait a few moments". That is, you are provided with two options. Assuming that you have a press button unit you press the starred button. You then hear the message "Metéo France Savoie". Press button one for the departmental forecast, two for the mountain forecast, or three for the agricultural forecast. Evidently you will press two; nor is it necessary to wait for the end of the message before doing this. The forecast then follows. If, however, you do not have a press button unit and have to wait after the first message, you will hear after a pause "Pronounce the word STOP after the tone which follows the description of the forecast required". Again, it is the second tone that you need. Note that the general number 36 68 02 —, where the last two figures are the number of the department, will obtain the weather forecast for any department from anywhere in France. Thus 73 gives you Savoie, 74 gives Haute Savoie, 38 gives Isère, 01 gives Ain, etc.

NOTE: In spring 1996, France Telecom will be changing the eight-figure telephone numbers to ten-figure numbers. This will mean that all eight-figure numbers given here, ie. for all correspondents in France, should then be preceded by 04. For calls outside France, the international code will change from 19 to 00. It is not known at this time with certainty what will happen to the number on which the weather forecast is given. This is a special number starting with 36 68 and will probably become 0836 68.... The police number will probably remain 17.

Key to Maps

These have been kept as simple as possible and the following symbols are used:

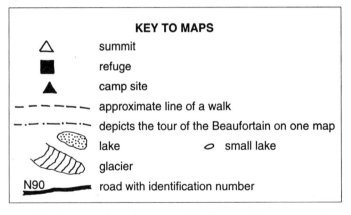

Altitudes are given in metres. For those still accustomed to thinking in terms of feet, the conversion is $1m = 3^{1}/_{4}ft$.

Distances are given in kilometres since this is the measure used on the continent. Conversion to miles is calculated from the relation 5 miles = 8km. Note that ridges are shown by thick black lines but that a thick black line may in certain cases indicate the edge of an escarpment.

CHAPTER 1

Around the Col de la Madeleine

INTRODUCTION

The Col de la Madeleine road connects the Tarentaise and Maurienne valleys from the N90 near La Léchère to La Chambre on the N6 just north of St Jean de Maurienne. It is a narrow road which has recently been improved and gives access to the Massif de la Lauzière and to one route up the Cheval Noir on its south side. The Lauzière are unique in the region in being the only hills formed from igneous rocks and the scenery is in parts reminiscent of Scotland. The massif is increasing in altitude by some 1.8mm per annum and it is estimated that in half a million years or so it will be approaching the present altitude of Mt Blanc.

As will be seen from the map, the Lauzière ridge runs in a more or less straight line between the Tarentaise and Maurienne valleys. The highest peak, the Grand Pic de la Lauzière (2829m), is climbed up a small glacier in its north-facing combe and so is outside the scope of this guide. The whole ridge is very crenellated and its rocky spikes are very imposing when seen from the surrounding hills. The eastern slopes of the main ridge send down a series of spurs towards the Madeleine road, each enclosing a steep valley, and the walks follow these to cols, lakes or summits. The valleys are short, and it is a characteristic of the Lauzière that the walks are short but very steep. Access is facilitated by two side roads which zig-zag up the ends of the spur ridges and take you well above the forest line. The area is very quiet in summer and you will tend to be alone on these hills. This contrasts with the winter season when each of the side valleys may contain up to a hundred people making the climb on skis. The topography on the western slopes is similar to that of the eastern ones but they are much more extensively forested and so more difficult of access. The view towards the main glaciated mountains of the region is also much more imposing from the open, eastern slopes.

South-east of the Col de la Madeleine is a cirque which seems to

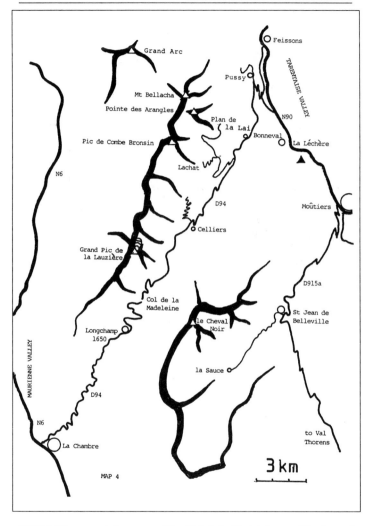

MAP 4. The mountains around the Col de la Madeleine and the layout of the road system

have no collective name but has as its culminating point the Cheval Noir (2832m), which is much climbed by parties, often with accompagnateurs, from St Francis Longchamp. The east-facing cirque is very attractive and is well provided with flora in season. It is reached via a narrow road which climbs in zig-zags through the village of St Jean de Belleville and then follows a valley through the hamlet of Deux Nants as far as La Sauce. This in itself is a very pleasant drive which could well make a satisfactory picnic outing. The river running through this valley is the Nant Brun and Deux Nants is where two streams meet, both names with evident Welsh affinities. The Cheval Noir is quite isolated in its position and this gives it more stature than its height might suggest. It is not always evident how it came by its name - the Black Horse - but if seen from the direction of Bourg St Maurice with the lighting in silhouette in the evening sky, the outline of a dark horse's head held high is unmistakable.

The whole of the region is covered by D&R Map No.11 except for part of Walk No.4. Two TOP25 maps are needed: 3432ET for Walks 1, 3, 4 and 5 and 3433ET for Walks 2 and 6 (the Cheval Noir).

1: Col du Loup and Lac Freydon

Grade:	2 to col, 3 to lac
Map:	3432ET
Time needed:	50min to col with height gain 150m; 1h 30min to lac
Height gain:	350m (total)
Comment:	A pleasant walk to a tiny tarn situated in a magnificent craggy cirque

Approach: Drive towards the Col de la Madeleine from the N90 main road and climb past Bonneval. Shortly after Bonneval, the road swings into a side valley, across its river and back to the slopes of the main valley. At this point a junction on the right appears with little warning and this should be followed. A surfaced and reasonable, though narrow, road now climbs through the forest. Keep left at the first junction and continue past Le Biollay and La Pautaz (situated just below the road) to a second junction, where again go left and climb a series of hairpins until nearly at the farm of Lachat. At the

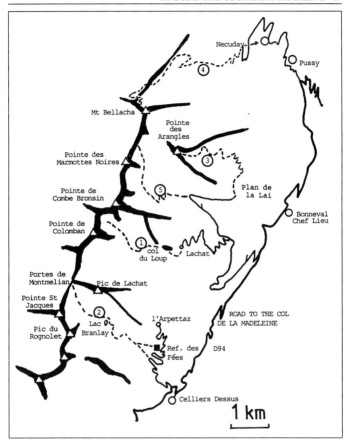

MAP 5. The northern part of the Chaine de la Lauzière with the lines followed by walks Nos. 1 to 5. The tarn at the end of walk No. 1 is too small to show

last bend before the farm there is parking and a signpost.

Ascent: The map shows a complex of paths behind Lachat which are mostly, I think, herdsmen's tracks. There is a gently rounded moorland dome behind the farm which is cut away sharply on its

55

southern side, where it falls steeply to the Colomban Valley below. Walk up to the farm and cross the dome towards this edge and follow paths which run parallel to it and eventually start to descend to the valley below. Avoid this and keep right, aiming for the rocky ridge ahead. The path is not immediately evident but once you are on the ridge can be followed easily to where it descends to the Col du Loup.

From the left of the col an obvious path traverses a steep, grassy hillside to meet another path which climbs from the Colomban Valley. Continue up the stream and head towards the top of the combe on a path which rapidly fades out. Climb via a series of grassy slopes and ledges, keeping generally to the right until the little tarn is reached. The place is marked on the map as "Chalets de Freydon" though these seem to have disappeared.

Descent: By the same route.

2: The Portes de Montmélian (2459m)

Grade:	3
Map:	3433ET
Time needed:	2h 30min
Height gain:	750m
Comment:	A short steep walk whose main merit is the view from the col. This is named "les Portes de Montmélian" because it is possible to see right down the valley to the entrance to the Combe de Savoie with the hills of the Bauges behind

Approach: Drive towards the Col de la Madeleine from La Léchère. There are a couple of hairpin bends at Celliers Dessus and just after the second, a narrow road goes off to the right. This is followed to the sixth (right-hand) hairpin bend where there is parking. An alternative starting point is the Refuge des Fées further up this road.

Ascent: An obvious path takes you up into the valley beyond, past a ruined chalet and through a little gully where it crosses the stream. It then climbs the steep slope ahead to arrive on a rim overlooking the lake called le Branlay. This is a pleasant spot for a picnic, though the lake may well have dried up in hot weather. Continue around the rim to the right and across and up the slopes beyond. There are traces of a path which lead towards a little gully and follow this to a series of level areas. Continue up and tend right until you are on the neck of the ridge which connects the main ridge with the Pic de Lachat. Turn left and climb the last slopes onto the main ridge at its lowest point.

Descent: By the same route.

3: Pointe des Arangles (2344m)

Grade:	3
Map:	3432ET
Time needed:	2h 40min
Height gain:	690m
Comment:	A short but sharp ascent up a scenic valley to a peak with a magnificent panorama of the peaks of the Lauzière and of the whole of the glaciated peaks of the Tarentaise and Vanoise as well as Mt Blanc

Approach: As for Walk No.1 except that you go right at the second junction and drive to the parking spot at Plan de la Lai.

Ascent: A green track crosses the meadow above the parking area. Follow this up two steep sections and tend right after the second on a well marked footpath. This descends a little and traverses across the head of a valley, then climbs again to another meadow. Above you on the left is a green slope which is bordered on its left by scree and on its right by alder scrub. The path zig-zags up this green slope, though the approach path is not clear from below and you may have to climb until you find it. This climb leads to easy ground which is crossed to the Chalet de l'Arc over on the right.

The chalet is situated at the foot of a bank and a path appears to traverse left from the building. In fact, this is where the pipe for the water supply has been interred and should be ignored. Instead, walk to the left below the bank until a green rake is seen climbing up acutely right. Follow this and then turn left along the crest of the bank to reach some herd paths which climb through the steep ground ahead, keeping some cliffs to the left. When the slope eases, go right to a little col with a view of Pussy and surrounding villages almost straight below. To the left is a little pool while behind will be seen a grassy ridge which climbs to the foot of a small, stone-filled gully. Go to the foot of the gully where there are herd paths which climb to its right and bring you onto the shoulder of the mountain. Follow this using the ground between rock outcrops until you reach the summit some 300m further on. A pinnacle ridge runs north-west from the summit and points to the Bellacha and its rocky slopes, making a very fine view.

Descent: By the same route.

4: Mt Bellacha (2484m)

Grade:	4
Map:	3432ET
Time needed:	4h 20min
Height gain:	1300m
Comment:	This is the most northerly peak of the Lauzière and is an excellent viewpoint. The starting point is relatively low so that the walk involves a significant ascent for a not too high peak

Approach: Take the road to the Col de la Madeleine from La Léchère or Feissons. At the seventh hairpin there is a road off right signposted to Pussy which is followed through the village, below Necuday and on to Les Foyères. A track goes off sharp right here and zig-zags a short distance above the hamlet, then traverses to a bend where there is parking.

Ascent: Continue up the track a short distance until a newly made track is reached climbing steeply on the right. Follow this through the forest. It eventually turns into a path (though this may be widened to a track in the future) and traverses onto open hillside and to the Chalet de Fraitière. The path continues for about 200m then turns sharply right and traverses a tongue of the forest, though in the region of the bend the path is not well traced. A left-hand bend brings you onto open hillside again and shortly after to the Col de l'Arc. Just before the col you pass a stone-built shooting cabin. From the col, a ridge rises on the left and a path follows the line of this but below its summit rocks, with the ridge on the right. Steep ground is climbed to the crest of the ridge and this is followed a little way, any difficulties being avoided by taking paths which traverse to the right of the crest. A path is then followed which traverses right across steep grass to a little shoulder, then zig-zags up on the left to arrive abruptly just to the right of the summit. This is adorned with a strange metallic structure on which is written the name of the summit so that there can be no mistake as to where you are.

Descent: By the same route. Note that on the TOP25 map a footpath is shown which comes up via the Col de l'Homme and offers a way down. Much of this path is a figment of someone's imagination and no attempt should be made to follow it as in one place it descends a little cliff!

5: Combe des Marmottes Noires, Mt de la Perrière (2436m) and Mt Bellacha (2484m)

Grade:	4
Map:	3432ET
Time needed:	3h 10min
Height gain:	913m
Comment:	This is a very pleasant walk which climbs a splendid little valley below the Bellacha and the Pointe des Arangles. Rock walls and spiky ridges fall from the Pointe de Combe Bronsin and one climbs past these to the main ridge of the Lauzière with a good view of the Grand Arc and, in the distance, the Combe de Savoie. Possibly a better walk than No.2 but somewhat more difficult. A path is marked red on the map leading into the combe but this is non-existent, though the line can be followed with difficulty, and is in places dangerously exposed. I have commented on this non-existent path in the previous walk (No.4)

Approach: Drive in the direction of the Plan de la Lai as described for Walk No.3. After the junction with the road to Lachat has been passed, the road traverses into a valley and makes a sharp hairpin bend right, across a bridge. Park just before the bridge.

Ascent: Looking up the valley you can see that this is closed by a steep wall of rock and grass. To the left of the stream is an open hillside with a line of alder scrub defining the path of a stream which flows down from the rocks on the left. Make for this line of bushes. There is some path to help but only a trace will be found higher up. As you approach the stream, bear left and a good path will appear which leads up steep ground through the alder scrub. The path is used for taking stock to the pastures above and zig-zags up at a reasonable angle until it traverses right across the stream and peters out on easy ground above the wall blocking the valley. This path approximates to the route shown by a black dashed line on the TOP25 map.

The chalet of Les Pissus is visible over on the right and the valley ahead is again blocked by another wall of rough ground. Walk over uneven ground past some ruins and then climb using the herd tracks where possible but keeping left under a little cliff and making for the ridge behind the Pointe des Marmottes Noires. The going is steep at times, mostly on grass, and the paths are not always helpful. The crest of the ridge itself is mostly easy and can be followed for some way in the direction of Mt Bellacha, whose metallic crown can be seen easily from here. Eventually go right and make for an obvious path which crosses the end of the ridge ahead. Once around the right-hand corner, it is possible to climb to the narrow summit ridge of the Mont de la Perrière and/or continue to the Bellacha.

Descent: Necessarily by the same route, traversing back round the upper part of the combe. Avoid the temptation to descend into the floor of the combe, where there are obvious sheep paths, as this inevitably leads you to the upper wall blocking the valley. It is possible to descend but the problem is to find a workable route.

6: The Cheval Noir (2832m)

Grade:	4
Map:	3433ET
Time needed:	4h
Height gain:	1212m
Comment:	The route described is the longest but also, I believe, the most attractive approach to this isolated mountain. There is an alternative route from the Col de la Madeleine via the Col du Cheval Noir which involves only 940m of ascent but which I have not done in summer

Approach: Drive from Moûtiers towards Val Thorens on a good road, typical of the road to a major ski resort. At the village of St Jean de Belleville there is a signpost to La Sauce. Take this road which zig-zags up through the village then follows the side of the valley of the Nant Brun through the hamlets of Deux Nants and La Sauce. This is a delightful valley and makes a very pleasant approach to the mountain. At La Sauce the road becomes a track which climbs beside the stream to a junction and a bridge. Park here or a little lower by the hamlet.

Ascent: Follow the track to the right as far as the second hairpin bend. Turn left on a track which has recently been improved and follow this towards the Chalets de la Platière. Just below the chalets, a signpost directs you right on a traverse across a convex slope to pick up herd paths up the valley, which runs almost due north from here. At first keep the stream on your left and make a fairly steep ascent over grassy slopes with only occasional traces of path. The valley steepens and at this point it is advantageous to cross the stream, when a definite path will be found on its other bank. This leads to a level step in the valley from where the path climbs on the right by a stream. The slope eases again and then steeper slopes lead to the Col du Cheval Noir at the head of the valley. The path is not well marked but on the col, one meets the much used path from la Madeleine. Follow this to the right. It climbs the ridge at first, then traverses right into a combe below the summit. Here it turns steeply up the mountain for a while, then swings left, the slope eases and

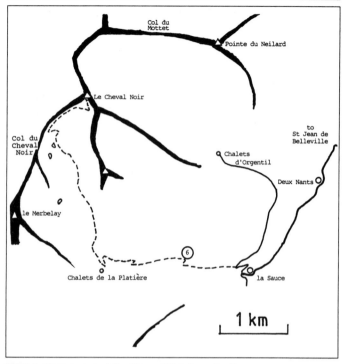

MAP 6. The ascent of the Cheval Noir from La Sauce

you are on the summit. This is quite extensive and gives a grandstand view of the Lauzière, the Tarentaise and Vanoise hills and, to the south, the big mountains of the Dauphiné Alps. Also, beside the route to the Col du Glandon, is the glacier of the Pic de l'Étandard.

Descent: By the same route.

SOME SHORT WALKS

1. **Lac du Loup** - From the parking place near Lachat described in Walk No.1, follow the signposts and descend herd paths which traverse left into a little valley whose head is formed by the Col du Loup. Continue up this valley and over a lip to find the lake, which

is a popular picnic spot. This involves some 50m of climbing. - *Grade 2*

2. **Le Branlay** - This is the first part of Walk No.2 with 300m of ascent on a good path. - *Grade 2*

3. **Le Lacte and the Grand Plan** - Le Lacte is a small lake near L'Arpettaz above the Refuge des Fées (Walk No.2). One can approach closely by car and use as a picnic place. It is possible to walk up the slopes behind the lake to a point marked as 2127m - about 170m ascent - then descend behind to a shallow col where you turn right and follow the hillside down and round back to Le Lacte. - *Grade 2*

4. **Plan de la Lai** - This is the start of Walk No.3 and is a very pleasant spot for a picnic with walks possible in the forest around.

INTRODUCTION

Méribel and Courchevel are both large ski resorts and are two of the famed "Trois Vallées" complex, Val Thorens being the third. Both resorts are surrounded by ski uplift equipment but as one moves south towards the area of the Vanoise National Park, this is left behind and wild country is to be found. Pralognan is also a ski resort but relatively modest and is effectively surrounded by the Park so that its development has been restricted. It is sited among some of the most magnificent scenery to be encountered in this part of the Alps, and is worth visiting on that score alone. The group of resorts is situated very much in the centre of the hen of Savoy and is reached from Moûtiers by a good road which climbs steadily to Bozel, passing the forks for Méribel and Courchevel on the way. After Bozel, the road climbs in steps to Pralognan, turning to the south as it does so. At Pralognan you come face to face with the great rock walls of the Grand Marchet and the Roc de la Valette which buttress the Glacier de la Vanoise beyond.

To the right, a long and relatively straight valley cuts deep into the hills, pointing a little west of south, and gives access to the mountains dividing it from Courchevel and Méribel. The Glacier de la Vanoise defines the eastern side of this valley. It is possible to drive on a surfaced road as far as the Pont de la Pêche where there is extensive parking, though this is generally full by late morning. There are several cols over the ridge which forms the western side of the valley and good footpaths lead over to Courchevel and Méribel. The ridge culminates at the head of the valley in the twin peaks of the Aiguille de Polset and the Aiguille de Péclet and their surrounding glaciers, the whole often being referred to as "Péclet-Polset". The head of the valley is closed by the Col de la Chavière (2796m) and a path over this col leads to the Maurienne and down

Notre Dame des Vernettes below the cliffs of the Aiguille Rousse

The Aiguille Rousse from the Aiguille Grive. The path at the top of the Col d'Entreporte can be seen just below the parapenter. The Punurin Valley lies far below.

The Pas de l'Ane, looking towards the Combe de Savoie

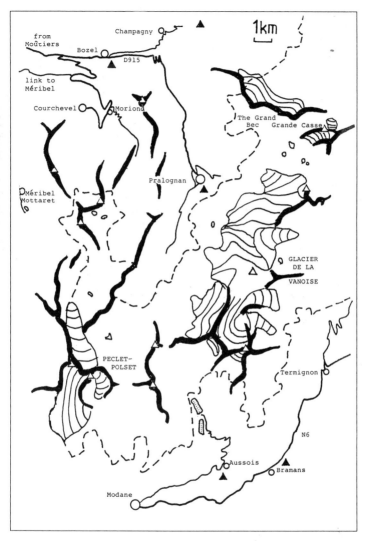

MAP 7. The mountains around Pralognan and the access roads, including those in the Maurienne. The dashed line shows the limits of the Vanoise National Park, which encloses all the major massifs

to Modane. There are no exits on the east as these are blocked by the long wall supporting the Glacier de la Vanoise, not at least until it is possible to skirt the south of the glacier, via the high Col d'Aussois (2916m) which takes you behind the magnificent slabs of the Pointe de l'Échelle which overhang the approach to the Col de la Chavière. The Col d'Aussois is one of the high points of the tour of the Glacier de la Vanoise; indeed this path parallel to the valley following a series of high balconies.

Looking left as you approach Pralognan, there is a steep valley which climbs towards the Col de la Vanoise, though this is divided into two by the blade of rock known as the Aiguille de la Vanoise and either side provides an interesting ascent. Ahead is the Grande Casse which at 3855m is the highest peak in this region of the Alps. It is climbed most easily using the Glacier des Grands Couloirs which descends towards the col from the summit. The actual summit is to the left of the glacier and the subsidiary summit to the right is known as the Pointe Mathews after the Englishman and his guides who first climbed the mountain in September 1860. The Col de la Vanoise is surrounded, both to the north and to the south, by high craggy summits and glaciers, and the only way over leads to the valley of the Leisse and hence either to the Maurienne again, or to Val d'Isère and Tignes.

We will deal first with the excursions using Pralognan as a centre and then link these with those possible from Courchevel and Méribel.

The majority of the walks are covered by the TOP25 Map 3534OT but Map 3633ET is needed for the eastern side of the tour du Glacier de la Vanoise. D&R Map No.11 covers the whole area needed.

1: Col de la Vanoise (2516m)

Grade:	2 by the Lac des Vaches, 3 via the Arcelin track
Map:	3534OT
Time needed:	3h 10min
Height gain:	872m
Comment:	There are two possible approaches to the col, one either side of the Aiguille de la Vanoise, and it is

appropriate to make this a circular walk, the more so since the two routes are very different. The scenery is everywhere quite magnificent: the cliffs of the Grand Marchet and the Arcelins, the rocks of the Aiguille de la Vanoise, a close-up of the Grande Casse, and the glaciated peaks and moraines north of the curious Lac des Vaches. Food can be purchased at the refuge on the col

Approach: At a roundabout near the entrance to Pralognan there is a road off which crosses the river. Take this and follow signs to Les Fontanettes, though the signs are not always clear. A good surfaced road traverses the slopes above the town and reaches the hamlet of Les Fontanettes, where there is adequate parking. It is also possible to continue a little further on a track to the right which leads to other parking places and a bridge (1676m).

Ascent: You can go up by the Arcelin track and return by the lac. Walk to and cross the bridge turning immediately left and so uphill.

Looking back near the top of the Arcelin path. The Grand Marchet is on the left and Petit Mt Blanc is in the distance centred in the 'V' of the valley

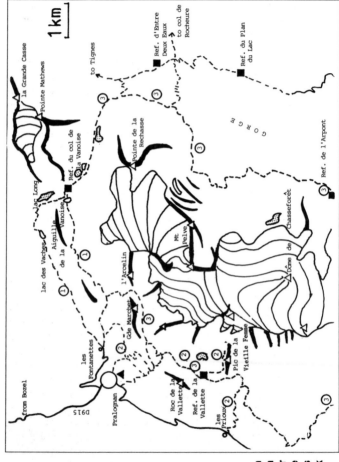

MAP 8. Pralognan and the northern half of the Glacier de la Vanoise showing the lines taken by walk Nos. 1 to 3

Follow the track until it starts to swing to the left around a cirque and look for a path which leaves on the right and climbs a gently sloping moraine. This leads to an obvious rocky gully and sets out to climb this. A junction of paths, furnished with a signpost, is quickly reached where it is necessary to take the left-hand branch, which traverses out over a rocky prow and then climbs for a short distance along ledges at the top of an exposed little cliff. (The right-hand branch climbs steeply towards the Cirque du Dard above on a path which is difficult but never dangerous. If time permits, this is a worthwhile deviation to approach the obvious waterfall or to look at the rocks of the Petite Aiguille de l'Arcelin. *Grade 4.*) A good path meanders its way upwards over varied ground with first the Moriond hill and then the Aiguille de la Vanoise on the left. Eventually, easier ground is reached which leads to the Col de la Vanoise. The Lac des Assiettes is usually dry! From the col, in addition to those mountains already mentioned, one can see the Pointe de la Réchasse due south. This and the Glacier de l'Arcelin form the northernmost point of the Glacier de la Vanoise.

Descent: Take a good path which goes more or less north from the refuge and near but above the shore of Lac Long and skirts the eastern end of the Aiguille de la Vanoise. You quickly reach the foot of an enormous moraine heap which has been deposited by the Glacier de la Grande Casse and on which *Campanula cenisia* can be discovered in August. The path continues steeply down until it reaches the shore of the Lac des Vaches. This lake, while quite extensive at perhaps 300m by 200m, is nowhere more than about a foot deep but avoids being dried up because its water is continually replenished by seepage from the moraine. It is more like a very wide stream than a lake. It is crossed on a causeway of flat rocks which have been laid straight across the centre. Thereafter, the path descends steadily, crosses the Pont de la Glière and so into the forest and almost straight down to Les Fontanettes.

Alternative: It is possible to take the cable-car from Pralognan to Mont Bochor. Go round the knoll behind the cable-car station and follow paths down to the right and then take a left fork on a path which traverses to the Lac des Vaches path. The view from Mont Bochor is remarkable but if the return is made via the Arcelin path it is necessary to descend all the way to Pralognan on foot.

2: Pic de la Vieille Femme (2738m)

Grade:	3 or 4 to Refuge de la Vallette depending on route chosen; 4 to summit
Map:	3534OT
Time needed:	4h 30min by the Isertan and Pas de l'Âne or 3h 20min from Les Prioux. The descent to Les Prioux requires 2h and should be used regardless of the route used for the ascent. Les Prioux to Pralognan requires 50min
Height gain:	1318m maximum
Comment:	This walk can be accomplished either as a circuit or as a shorter trip starting at Les Prioux using the same route for both ascent or descent, though this misses out the magnificent Pas de l'Âne section of path. The scenery is everywhere impressive

Approach: Drive to Pralognan. The town centre has been made into a one-way system and the road signs will direct you towards the skating rink used for curling contests in the Olympic Games. Park near here if you intend to do the full circuit. If you have two cars leave one here and the other at Les Prioux up the Doron de Chavière. If you are doing the shorter ascent, park at Les Prioux.

Ascent - full circuit: The road into Pralognan crosses a small bridge and just prior to this a lane goes right, to the campsite. From here one can go either left or right then climb straight up to join the Sentier Nanette in the Forêt d'Isertan. The left-hand version is possibly the better one and leads to an impressive viewpoint. From here, the path climbs through forest and gives a view of the Cascade du Grand Marchet. Beware a couple of false paths which lead off to the left. The path then traverses over open hillside and meets the other path from the campsite.

From here the route leads steeply up to the Pas de l'Âne which comprises a scramble up rocks in an open gully, not too difficult but impressive enough, to reach easier ground below the Petit Marchet. During this ascent, two paths are passed which go left into the Cirque du Grand Marchet, whose scenery is well worth a detour, preferably by the upper path as otherwise you miss all the fun of the steep part of the Pas de l'Âne. You then climb to the Roc du Tambour. The angle eases and the path leads to the Refuge de la Vallette. On the immediate left is the Dôme des Sonnailles and the ice cliffs which form the edge of the Glacier de la Vanoise hanging over steep rock walls. Water streams down from the dôme over rock into the Lac de la Vallette, whose outlet disappears mysteriously into a hole below the path, to re-emerge in some unknown location. The refuge provides excuse for a pause and refreshment.

As you approach the refuge, the Pic de la Vieille Femme can be seen behind and to the left, in the form of a low ridge which, despite its altitude, is dwarfed by the walls behind which support the Glacier de la Vanoise. From the refuge it is a simple matter to climb up the nearest end of the ridge and then scramble along to the highest point. Apart from the pleasures of the climb, the ridge is also the home to numerous plants of *Primula viscosa* whose purple-pink flowers brighten the rocks towards the end of July. One can return to the refuge by the same way or descend near the summit on the left and return passing the ruins of a previous refuge.

Descent: Continue in a southerly direction from the refuge. There are two paths, which meet eventually and descend to the ruined Chalet des Nants where there is a fork. Take the right-hand path which leads steadily down to Les Prioux. The path crosses the stream then traverses left more than seems necessary but in so doing avoids some difficult ground on the right. The road at Les Prioux takes you back to Pralognan. It is possible to miss out the two last hairpin bends by taking a path which descends on the right between walls. Do not cross the river, as the map suggests, but turn left with the river on your right on a path which takes you back to the road. If you are camping, however, then it is of course better to use the path on the other side of the river.

Alternative ascent: Set out from and return to Les Prioux. Height gain reduced to 1027m.

Alternative ascent: Drive to Les Fontanettes as described for Walk No.1. Follow the track to the bridge over the river and turn sharp right. The track descends gently until a square shaft with a grid on top is reached where you take a path which goes off on the left. This is not too evident at first but quickly improves and follows a pleasant traverse with views to the Cascade de la Fraiche, eventually joining the Sentier Nanette. This variation reduces the amount of ascent but extends the walk, particularly at the end of the day when it is necessary to climb from Pralognan to Les Fontanettes to get back to the car.

3: Tour du Glacier de la Vanoise

Grade: Mostly an easy 3 but with some sections of 4, notably the Col du Grand Marchet or the Pas de l'Âne, depending on the start chosen, and the ascent to the Col d'Aussois

Maps: 3534OT and 3633ET

Time needed: This is a long tour which will take four days and require three nights in refuges

Comment: This is a magnificent tour which in many ways stands comparison with the Tour of Mt Blanc. It is shorter but goes higher at the Col d'Aussois and never descends below 2000m other than at the start/end. The path - which is everywhere excellent - thus keeps uncompromisingly above the forest line and you remain firmly in a mountain environment for the whole walk. The scenery is everywhere breathtaking, with views across the surrounding valleys on one side and up to the glacier icecap on the other. It is also possible to ascend one minor peak on the tour, the Pointe de l'Observatoire (3015m) above the Col d'Aussois. The walk can be undertaken in either direction but is described in the anticlockwise direction. Note that the refuges should be booked in advance

Approach: Park either at Les Fontanettes, as described for Walk No.1, or if starting via the Pas de l'Âne, around Pralognan.

First day: Pralognan to the Refuge de la Vallette
There are two good alternative starts, one via the Cirque du Dard

and one via the Pas de l'Âne, the latter being the way described in the French booklet published by the Vanoise National Park Authorities, *Le Tour des Glaciers du Vanoise*. Note that the first day is given in this booklet as going as far as the Refuge du Génépy, which was situated above Montaimont and is marked on quite recent maps. This refuge no longer exists as it was swept away by a winter avalanche.

Time needed: Via Cirque du Dard, 5h 25min; via Pas de l'Âne, 4h 40min

Height gain: For the first alternative in two stages of 846m then 380m, making 1226m in all and 1244m for the second

Cirque du Dard: Walk up to the Cirque du Dard as described for Walk No.1. Once into the cirque, with the steep rocks of the Petit Aiguille de l'Arcelin to one side and those of the Grand Marchet to the other, it is possible to see a col high on the right, behind the Grand Marchet. The path goes over this col and is evident in the scree ahead, though the last pull just below the col is a steep scramble.

This is the Col du Grand Marchet. A good path descends into the magnificent Cirque du Grand Marchet and leads to a level grassy place beside the stream. Here, a path junction is encountered and you take the left-hand fork which climbs around the lower slopes of the Petit Marchet to reach a second path junction. Again keep left. You are now on the Pas de l'Âne path described in Walk No.2; follow this to the refuge. After checking in with the guardian, there may also be time to scramble up the Pic de la Vieille Femme. The views from here and from the Col du Tambour are splendid. The Grand Marchet with the Grande Casse behind, the Grand Bec above Pralognan and, across the valley, the Aiguille de May and Petit Mt Blanc are but a fraction of the peaks visible.

The alternative first day is to climb from the municipal campsite at Pralognan via the Pas de l'Âne as described for Walk No.2.

Second day: From La Vallette to the Fond d'Aussois
This is a long day and involves crossing the highest part of the route. An early start is therefore essential.

Time needed: 7h 35min plus 35min for the Pointe de l'Observatoire

Height gain: 360m then 716m to the col. The Pointe de l'Observatoire is another 100m higher. Total ascent 1176m

A good path descends from La Vallette as far as the Chalet des Nants where the path comes up from Les Prioux. Keep left and follow a path which traverses the hillside, making a gentle descent until just above Montaimont. Keep high here and follow the path which climbs the hillside to the left and leads onto the crest of a ridge. This leads you into the Cirque du Génépy (not named as such on the map) dominated by the Dôme de l'Arpont, and then climbs gently towards the foot of the moraine of the Glacier du Génépy. The moraine is steep and the path zig-zags arduously upwards until it is possible to traverse right below the Point Ariande and follow another balcony section of the walk. The path descends gently around the end of the crenellated Crête de l'Argentine and reaches a level area in the valley above the hamlet of Ritort.

Continue up this valley on a path which rapidly steepens and attack the slopes of the Col d'Aussois which rise on the right, presenting you with over 700m of ascent in something like 2^{1}/$_{2}$km. The upper slopes can be particularly awkward. There will inevitably be some névé though this will have been well beaten into a path by other walkers. Where the névé has melted, however, the path will be vestigial and progress has to be made up the uncovered scree slopes, following the best available line. The top of the col is wide and level and a welcoming place to make a well earned pause.

As you arrive at the summit of the col, the Pointe de l'Observatoire can be seen to the right. It is well worthwhile to climb this peak as the views around are exceptional. The rucksacks can be left near the col and a way made up the rocks to the top. There are no real difficulties and it is possible to scramble up almost anywhere. Indeed, it is quite likely that there will be many other walkers around with the same objective, all spread out over the side of the peak.

The summit is quite small and will only allow a few people at a time to gain the highest point. The western side of the peak is much more impressive than that just climbed and drops 800m to the

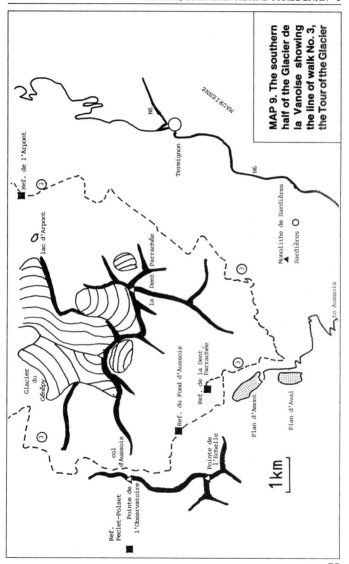

MAP 9. The southern half of the Glacier de la Vanoise showing the line of walk No. 3, the Tour of the Glacier

valley below with great slabs of rock falling steeply to scree. Directly across the valley is the moonscape of the Col du Soufre with the Lac Blanc below and the Péclet-Polset refuge. The lac is a milky colour and I have heard several explanations as to the reason for this - powdered rock in suspension or interaction between chemicals leached from the diversity of rocks around have both been suggested and perhaps both play a part. The peaks Péclet-Polset form an impressive background while along the ridge to the south the eye is led to the slabs of the Pointe de l'Échelle and in the far distance, the big mountains of the Dauphiné Alps. To the east can be seen the hunched shape of the Dent Parrachée which forms the southern limit of the Glacier de la Vanoise and is one of the higher mountains in this part of the Alps.

The descent from the col to the Fond d'Aussois is made over a series of rocky ledges and then grassy terrain to the bottom of the valley. The refuge is very pleasantly situated beside a stream at a point where the valley levels out for a while.

Third day: From the Fond d'Aussois to the Arpont
This is a shorter and much less arduous day on a balcony path which wanders up and down, keeping between 2500m and 2095m altitude.

Time needed: 5h 30min
Height gain: 653m in three stages

Follow the path from the Font d'Aussois towards the two reservoirs Plan d'Amont and Plan d'Aval (amont = to the mountain, or upper, and aval = to the valley, or lower). At the end of the valley you meet the long-distance footpath, the G.R.5, and stay with this until well into the following day. Take the left fork, keeping above the reservoirs which are thus on your right. There is parking by the upper reservoir and this explains the large number of walkers who may be encountered on the Col d'Aussois and who have come up for the day from the Maurienne. The junction with the path up to the Refuge de la Dent Parrachée is quickly reached at the foot of the Vallon de la Fournache, with a good view of another aspect of the Dent Parrachée at the head of the vallon. This refuge is an alternative to the Fond d'Aussois, though it is situated at a higher altitude. It is the starting point for ascents of the Dent Parrachée, the ordinary route starting up la Fournache.

Continue to traverse the hillside and at the next junction strike upwards, always keeping out of the valley. This is the most southerly point of the tour and from now onwards there will always be a northern element in the direction taken. About 2km further on there is a section marked as difficult on the maps. It is, indeed, quite a wild section but the only real difficulty involves a step over an open gully which cuts the path but which is well protected by a steel handrail. The hillside above is known as the Roc des Corneilles due to the small horn-like pinnacles which abound. In the forest below this section of the path is to be found the Monolithe de Sardières and this can be seen from certain vantage points. It is a great tooth of calcareous rock, 93m in height, and of easy access from the village of Sardières, much visited by tourists and rock climbers, for its ascent is difficult and challenging despite its relatively small stature among the giants of the surrounding mountains.

The path now zig-zags up the hillside and then takes a gently falling traverse, crossing the wide gully of the curiously named Ruisseau de Bonne Nuit and continues to the lowest part of the day's walk near Montafia and Le Mont. Glimpses of the Dent Parrachée will be had all along this section. It should also be mentioned that several paths descend to the Maurienne along this part of the route and all should be avoided. From here a stiffish climb leads to the Refuge de l'Arpont past attractive water slides. This refuge was built specially by the Park authorities in the early 1970s.

Fourth day: From the Arpont to the Col de la Vanoise and Les Fontanettes

This again is a straightforward balcony path which stays high, never descending below 2300m until you start to make the last descent from the Col de la Vanoise.

Time needed: 6h
Height gain: 512m in three stages. 900m descent

The path climbs quickly above the refuge in rocky terrain. A section ahead is again marked as difficult on the maps though the path is good and there seem to be no particular problems. The section is, nevertheless, quite exposed with a steep drop into the gorge of the Doron de la Rocheure some 700m below. If covered by névé, this section could be demanding. Less steep terrain is soon reached and then the highest point of today's part of the walk. A gentle descent follows into a great moraine-filled bowl into which spill several glaciers from the Vanoise icecap. Ahead are the rocks of Mont Pelve, the Roche de Foran and the Pointe de la Réchasse, the latter being the northernmost buttress of the Glacier de la Vanoise. To the left is the Dôme de Chasseforêt, the highest point of the icecap. Towards the far side of the moraine, the path crosses the stream called the Letta. This is a patois word for the whey obtained during cheesemaking and no doubt has much the same significance as the "Sourmilk Gills" of the English Lake District.

It is possible to follow the Letta up to the Lac de la Roche Ferran if time permits, and though I have not done this variation, it must be a very impressive place, nestled right under the rock cliffs of the mountain. The path now climbs a little between some small lakes and then continues its gentle descent to a junction above the chalets of La Para. Here we leave the G.R.5 and continue to traverse the hillside, with one steep descent and then a climb through immense blocks, some of which have been moved into position to form a rocky staircase. Another path junction and then a disused military blockhouse and the path gains easier ground and enters the high valley that runs between the enormous wall of the Pointe Mathews and the slopes of the Pointe de la Réchasse. A gentle but long climb now follows, passing several lakes and a couple of crosses until the Col de la Vanoise is reached. Here, the refuge can provide provisions and shelter if this is needed. The last descent to the valley is made either by the Lac des Vaches or by the Lac des Assiettes and the Arcelin path, as described for Walk No.1.

Summary of refuges

La Vallette - Altitude 2584m. Meals provided, 48 beds (79 08 00 70) (booking essential). Parc National de la Vanoise.

Fond d'Aussois - Altitude 2324m. Meals provided, 36 beds (79 20 32 87). Club Alpin Français.

Dent Parrachée - Altitude 2511m. Meals provided, 29 beds (79 20 32 87). Club Alpin Français.

Arpont - Altitude 2309m. Meals provided, 90 beds (79 20 51 51). Parc

National de la Vanoise.

Entre Deux Eaux - Altitude 2120m. Meals provided, 60 beds (79 20 50 24). Private. While off-route, this refuge provides alternative shelter.

Col de la Vanoise - Altitude 2516m. Meals provided, 156 beds (79 08 25 23). Club Alpin Français. A useful refuge if making the tour in the clockwise direction.

4: Col Rouge and Col and Pointe des Fonds (2731m, 2907m and 3024m)

Grade:	4, much scrambling involved with some slow going
Map:	3534OT
Time needed:	8h
Height gain:	1270m
Comment:	The central section of this walk, between the two cols and the descent towards the refuge of Péclet-Polset, is without any trace of footpath and should be undertaken only by a party capable of navigating by map. The route passes through some very wild country, and is an exacting tour

Approach: Drive through Pralognan and on in the direction of Les Prioux. Follow the road to its end at a parking site between Les Ruelles and Pont de la Pêche.

Ascent: Continue up the valley, over the bridge and follow the track passing the hamlet of Ritort, where a path leaves on the left making for the Col d'Aussois. About 500m further on a track leaves steeply on the right, signposted to the Col Rouge. The path zig-zags up steep scree at first and then the angle eases once entry is made into the Combe Rouge. Follow this to the col where eroded russet red rocks form a lunar landscape. To continue it is necessary to go either over or round the end of the ridge on the left, which descends to the north. The least arduous is to go over by scrambling over the slabby rocks on the left to the crest of the ridge and follow this south until a little gap is reached which enables a descent to be made into the bottom of the small valley which descends from the Col des Fonds. The Lac de Mont Coua is visible to the west. The valley is then

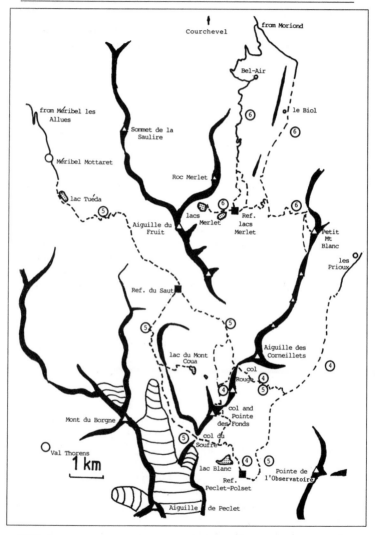

MAP 10. The mountains between Méribel/Courchevel and Peclet-Polset, showing the lines taken by walk Nos. 4 to 6

climbed to reach the col without any further difficulty.

The alternative, which involves a little more ascent overall, is to continue from the col on the path towards Méribel until it is possible to traverse left into the foot of the little valley which leads to the Col des Fonds. (This is in fact the route shown on the D&R map.) It should be remembered that this has a northern aspect and that extensive névé is likely early in the season. From the col, the ridge to the Pointe des Fonds goes up to the right as you approach the gap. It is followed to the summit, sometimes on the arête, sometimes on the scree and rocks just below on the right, and is a scramble all the way. The summit makes an excellent place for lunch in an exceptional mountain landscape.

Descend to the col by the same route and continue the walk by descending scree on the right towards the Péclet-Polset refuge. Go straight down at first and incline left towards a ridge which is visible below. Use this to lose height and then descend to the right over easier ground aiming for the path a little north of the Lac Blanc. There is no path through the scree but you are following, approximately, the ski route marked on the TOP25 map. Follow the path round the lac and over slabs to the refuge from where a well marked route takes you back down the valley to Pont de la Pêche and the car.

5: Col Rouge and Col du Soufre from Méribel
(2731m and 2819m)

Grade:	3
Maps	3534OT
Time needed:	8h 30min, plus 2h to refuge the evening before
Height gain:	605m then 800m, or 1405m in all
Comment:	This is a long circuit crossing two high cols but always on good paths among some very dramatic mountain scenery. Several variations are possible, including some shorter versions, and these will be summarised at the end of the section

Approach: Drive up to Méribel les Allues and on to Méribel Mottaret and through the tunnels there to the parking area.

Ascent to Refuge de la Saut: Continue along the track past Lac Tuéda and follow the main valley round to the left. Climb steeply up the zig-zags with the impressive rock architecture of the Aiguille du Fruit in front of you. At around 2000m in altitude you enter the Vallon du Fruit and the path climbs gently to the refuge.

Ascent to Col Rouge: There is an obvious fork in the valley evident from the refuge. The Col Rouge lies up the left-hand branch with a generally steep approach path which climbs 600m in 3km. Keep right at a junction at about 2352m. Cross the col and descend to the valley ahead. Turn right at the junction with the main valley path and climb again to the Refuge de Péclet-Polset. Climb a little to the north-west behind the refuge and follow the path around Lac Blanc and then steadily upwards to the Col du Soufre. The central section zig-zags up a steep rib. The names given the features are redolent of something a little out of the ordinary - Col and Roc du Soufre, Col du Grand Infernet - and this is certainly the case. The walker is surrounded by many eroded rocks of various hue which give a quite unreal effect, a moonscape even more impressive than that of the Col Rouge. You are also very close to the contrasting white and blue of the Glacier de Gebrulaz which flows from Péclet-Polset.

The path is now less well defined but the ground is easier. A moraine ridge separates you from the glacier on the left and the path goes around the northern end of this, under some small cliffs. Continue along the moraine parallel with the edge of the ice. You are not actually walking on the glacier itself but it is very close to you. The path continues to the foot of the glacier where it moves left to the centre of the valley and continues for some distance over a great field of moraine. A path is encountered going off on the right and can be seen climbing into a little gully on its way to Lac du Mont Coua. Continue past the moraine on a path which keeps high above the river to arrive at the Refuge du Saut and so descend to Lac Tuéda.

Alternatives: The Col du Soufre can be reached on a day's outing either from Lac Tuéda (allow 4h 10min for the 1120m ascent) or from the car park near the Pont de la Pêche described in Walk No.4 (allow 3h 40min for the 1055m ascent) and return by the same route.

The Lac du Mont Coua can also be reached in a day from Lac Tuéda and is a very pleasant place for a picnic (allow 3h 45min for the 970m ascent).

Summary of refuges

Le Saut - Altitude 2126m. Meals provided. 54 beds. Private.

Péclet-Polset - Altitude 2474m. Meals provided, 76 beds (79 08 72 13). Club Alpin Français.

6: Col de la Platta, Lacs Merlet and Petit Mt Blanc (2677m) from Courchevel

Grade:	2
Map:	3534OT
Time needed:	Col to Lacs Merlet 1h; to Petit Mt Blanc 2^{1}/2h. Total ascent on latter route 556m. If starting from the end of the surfaced road add 2h 20min for a climb of 700m
Comment:	As is common in most ski resorts there is a complex of paths among the uplift, which some will find disagreeable, and which in any case will be well documented in the local tourist office. The walks described here go further south and avoid the developed areas. The paths are in all cases good and have relatively gentle gradients except on the slopes of Petit Mt Blanc

Approach: Drive up to the ski resort of Courchevel 1650, which previously was known as Moriond. The road climbs into the village via a right-hand hairpin bend. Immediately after the road straightens out, a crossroads will be reached with a road going sharp left, up the hill. Take this road and follow up several hairpin bends until it levels out above the forest among a ribbon development of new housing, at an altitude of 1722m. There are now three options. The first is to drive to the Col de la Platta, where it is usual to find cars parked. Turn right on a side road in the middle of the housing and right again and take to a track which swings left and climbs the slopes ahead. This meanders its way to the restaurant and cable-car station at Mt Bel-Air, just before which a track goes off sharp right and takes you among ski uplift to the col. You can, of course, stop anywhere suitable along this track. The second option is to stop at the end of the surfaced road and continue on foot. A third possibility is to continue in the direction of the Vallée des Avals. The track is poor in places but it is possible to reach a parking place at an altitude of 1779m.

Ascents from Col de la Platta: For the Lacs Merlet, go south from the col and follow a path which traverses around the steep slopes of the Roc Merlet, avoiding a path which descends on the left and follows the boundary of the National Park. The path descends to the Refuge des Lacs Merlet (no guardian) and a little further on a branch right takes you quickly to the two lakes in the combe under the cliffs of the Aiguille de Fruit.

For Petit Mt Blanc de Pralognan, to give it its full title, we set out as above but take the left fork in the path and follow the National Park border down to the bottom of the valley. Now go east past the Chalets de la Grande Val and make for the Col des Saulces from where a path to the right takes you to the summit. This is a very popular mountain, as the number of paths which lead to it will testify. The summit is rounded and from a distance its shape reminds me of Great Gable in the Lake District, though not its colour, which is very light. On close acquaintance, the summit and slopes of this mountain are most unusual with ravines and craters eroded in the whitish rock. This is an example of a mountain made from gypsum. Pralognan seems to be almost at your feet and the icecap of the Glacier de la Vanoise dominates the opposite side of the Chavière Valley.

Ascent from Vallée des Avals: The track continues to Le Biol and on to the Chalets de la Grande Val from where you can climb to Petit Mt Blanc as described, or to the Lacs Merlet using a steepish short cut which takes you directly from the valley to the refuge.

It is possible to visit both the lakes and the Petit Mt Blanc in one day. If the car has been left down the valley, at the end of the road, the walk can be made a circuit, for instance Col de la Platta - Lacs Merlet - Petit Mt Blanc - Le Biol.

Descent: Otherwise use the route of the ascent. It is also worthwhile to vary the descent of the Petit Mt Blanc by dropping to the Col du Mône before traversing back to the Col des Saulces.

Lac de Mt Coua

SOME SHORT WALKS

The tourist offices at Méribel and Courchevel will supply plenty of suggestions and there is no need to repeat these here. At Pralognan I suggest:

1.   Go to Les Fontanettes (Walk No.1) and start as if to go up the Arcelin route but instead follow the track that swings around left through the **Bois de la Glière** and return via the first path on the left. About 200m ascent and descent. - *Grade 2*

2.   Descend from Les Fontanettes on a track which goes through the hamlet. You will eventually encounter a signpost to the **Cascade de la Fraiche**, which is well worth seeing. - *Grade 1*

3.   From Les Prioux in the Vallée de la Chavière, cross the river and follow a track down the valley to the **Pont de Gerlan** and return by the road. - *Grade 1*

4.   A more energetic excursion would be to visit the **Lacs des Vaches** using the return route described in Walk No.1 (700m height gain). - *Grade 2*

5.   The viewpoint above the **Sentier Nanette** is worth visiting but involves a steep climb of about 300m and should probably be classed *Grade 3.*

CHAPTER 3:

Between Bourg St Maurice andChampagny

INTRODUCTION

The hills between these two towns, Bourg in the north and Champagny in the south, form a wedge-shaped group with the point of the wedge to the west and the base in the east, along the last reach of the Tarentaise Valley. There are two high mountains, the Bellecôte, roughly in the centre, and Mont Pourri and its ridges on the eastern edge. There is also a big concentration of ski resorts: La Plagne with its satellite stations Montchavin, Montalbert and Champagny; Peisey-Nancroix; and on the same slopes, the much bigger Les Arcs - whose three centres are known by their altitudes, 1600, 1800 and 2000. Tignes is at the south-eastern corner of the wedge.

Because of this enormous concentration of uplift, you may think that the area might be spoiled from the point of view of the summer walker. However, much of the countryside around Mt Pourri, which at 3779m is the second highest mountain in the Tarentaise, is included in the Vanoise National Park, as is the terrain south-east of the Bellecôte, and there is some very attractive walking country even if not as extensive as in other parts of the region we describe.

This wedge of hills is divided into two parts. The first starts at the point of the wedge in the lower hills above the Croix de Feissons (above Môutiers) and increases in altitude as you move east to culminate in the summit of the Bellecôte (3417m). Beyond the Bellecôte, the wedge is cut into two by the deep valley of the Torrent du Ponturin whose source is in the high hills between Tignes and Bellecôte and runs to the valley via the Lac de la Plagne, Rosuel and Peisey. On the other side of this valley rises the isolated Mont Pourri with its long ridge to the south connecting with the glacier peak of the Dôme de la Sache. The G.R.5 long-distance footpath follows the valley of the Ponturin and crosses over to Tignes by the Col du Palet.

The major part of the area is covered by the TOP25 map No.3532ET, though omits a little of the valley of Champagny le Haut, for which No.3633ET is needed. D&R No.11 covers the whole

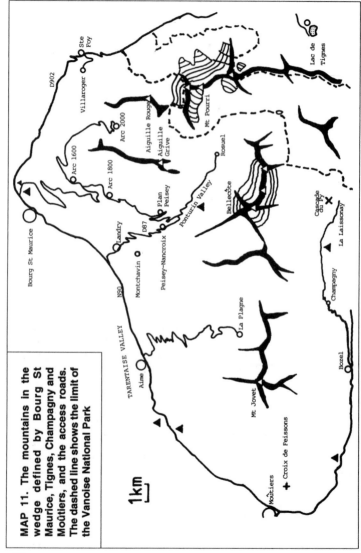

MAP 11. The mountains in the wedge defined by Bourg St Maurice, Tignes, Champagny and Moûtiers, and the access roads. The dashed line shows the limit of the Vanoise National Park

1km

area in question.

Two further points need to be made. The first is that the new TOP25 map includes a path which is described as the Tour de la Plagne. It is waymarked rather nattily by signs comprising a red bobble hat, which skiers will recognise. I have not investigated further but no doubt the tourist office at La Plagne will provide information. The second point is that there is a memorial at la Grand Plagne (or Plagne Centre) to a drop of arms made by the RAF at les Mines de la Plagne for the use of the French resistance.

1: Mt Jovet (2558m)

Grade:	3 from the north because paths are steep in places, 2 from the south
Map:	3532ET
Time needed:	3h 10min for northern circuit, as little as 40min from the south
Comment:	This is a good viewpoint with a "Table d'Orientation" on the summit, and makes a very pleasant outing. There is a good circular walk starting from the north or you can drive very close from the south. There is a refuge on the south side of the mountain, just below the summit. A network of paths to the east of the summit links with the La Plagne complex and allows the recommended walk to be extended

Northern circuit

Approach: Leave the main road at Aime and head for La Plagne. Before Macôt, amidst orchards, a road goes off right signposted to Longefoy. Follow this to and almost through the village and take a left fork for Montalbert. This turns out to be a wide, surfaced road and is followed past Montalbert and up to a series of holiday centres. At the last, a poor road goes up to the right with a sign "viabilité incertain". Take this and then the next right which is a track and climbs through forest passing a chair-lift several times and brings you out on a little hump above a deep valley. Descend a little, to around the Chalet de Prajourdan and park where convenient. You can, of course, start lower wherever parking is available.

Ascent: Continue on foot to a fork and take the right-hand track which traverses the east-facing side of the valley ahead. Two hairpin bends are passed and, just after the second, a narrow path climbs steeply up to the right. Follow the steep zig-zags of this to the Col du Lac (2359m) with its sharp summit ridge. Descend a little and traverse above the Lac du Signal, then climb into a little valley with a col at its head. At the col turn sharp right and follow the ridge to the summit of Mt Jovet.

Descent: A path follows the crest of a narrow ridge to your left as you arrive at the summit. Take this and traverse across the slopes below the little pyramids of the ridge, making for the Pas des Brébis. This is the first col to be reached and a path forks left and leads down into the combe below. Follow this to the floor of the combe and go left again, to pick up a track which leads past the Chalet des Étroits and a band of cliffs to join the track used on the ascent.

Approach from the south: Take the road which leaves the upper part of Bozel and traverses west across the hillside through the villages of Montagny, La Thuile and Feissons sur Salins. The tarmac ends here but the road continues as a track which winds its way up to the Croix de Feissons which is well worth a stop and is a good place for a picnic. The cross is erected on the top of a small bluff above steep wooded slopes and the town of Moûtiers seems almost directly below you. The track continues but there is a right fork which will take you eventually to the Refuge du Mont Jovet if you so wish. The secret is always to take the uppermost way at junctions and eventually you will drive out of the forest onto open hillside at about 2000m altitude. Park at any suitable place and walk, or else drive all the way to the refuge. Evidently, it is possible to vary the length of the walk, which in any case is not a long one. The summit is only some 200m above the refuge and is reached more or less directly on a good path.

Summary of refuges
Mt Jovet - Altitude 2350m. Meals provided. 134 beds (79 08 11 20). Club Alpin Français.

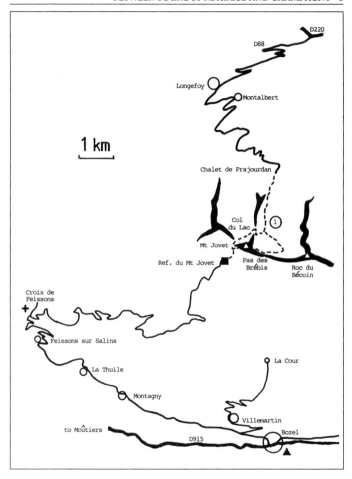

MAP 12. Access to Mt Jovet and walk No. 1

2: Lac de la Plagne (2144m)

Grade:	2
Map:	3532ET
Time needed:	2h 30min
Height gain:	588m
Comment:	This is a very pleasant walk along the upper valley of the Ponturin between Mt Pourri and the rocks of the Aliet, a satellite of the Bellecôte. From the lake it is possible to cross over either to Tignes via the Col du Palet (2652m) or to Champagny le Haut via the Col du Plan Séry (2609m). Both routes have good paths. The Col du Plan Séry goes via the Refuge de Plaisance and the Cascade du Py, which are described in the section dealing with short walks

Approach: From Landry, drive up to Peisey-Nancroix and continue up the valley to the end of the road at Rosuel. Here there is parking and a refuge.

Ascent: A track continues along the bottom of the valley but the path you need to follow makes a climbing traverse up the valleyside through alder scrub under the slopes of the Aliet. The path is very well defined as it is part of the G.R.5 long-distance footpath. It turns a corner under steep rocks then climbs more gradually into the level, upper part of the valley. Leave the G.R.5 at a right fork and descend a little over scree and so walk towards the lake. The Refuge of Entre le Lac is a little further on towards the Col du Plan Séry.

Descent from lac: Walk round the lake in an anticlockwise direction and climb a little to pick up the G.R.5 path and follow this back to Rosuel.

Summary of refuges
De Rosuel - Altitude 1556m. Meals provided. 64 beds (79 07 94 03). Parc National de la Vanoise.

3: Aiguille Grive and Col d'Entreporte (2732m)

Grade:	3; 4 from Arc 2000
Map:	3532ET
Time needed:	3h 40min from Plan Peisey
	2hr 30min from Arc 2000
Height gain:	1100m from Plan Peisey
	632m from Arc 2000
Comment:	The Aiguille Grive is the shapely, conical peak visible to the south-west from Bourg St Maurice, to the right of the ski resort of Arc 1800. Two routes of ascent are described which provide pleasant approaches to a mountain with a good viewpoint. The two walks can be combined into a traverse of the mountain if wished

Approach: From Landry, drive to Peisey-Nancroix. Just after the village the road goes right, then sharply left and a left fork will be seen just before the next bend. Follow this road to Plan Peisey and park near the shopping centre.

If making the ascent from Arc 2000, drive from Bourg St Maurice and park near the buildings of the ski resort. Alternatively, use the funicular (*funiculair*) and shuttle (*navette*) buses.

Ascent from Plan Peisey: A road goes off sharp right opposite the last shops of the upper arcade and passes under a chair-lift, near its loading stage. Continue past a restaurant and two hairpin bends on what is now a track. At the second, follow the track round to the right and climb gently over open slopes with the russet rock of the Aiguille Rousse ahead. The track eventually climbs abruptly to the little white church of Notre Dame des Vernettes in its magnificent setting under the Aiguille Rousse. The church's interior is well worth seeing if it is open. A path now crosses the slope to your left (with the Rousse behind you) to an open place below the forest where several paths meet.

Go right and climb steeply up through the woods until you reach open mountainside. Go right again and climb beside a little ridge, then descend slightly and cross steep, exposed slopes towards the Rousse. The path is good, though there is a short section over

93

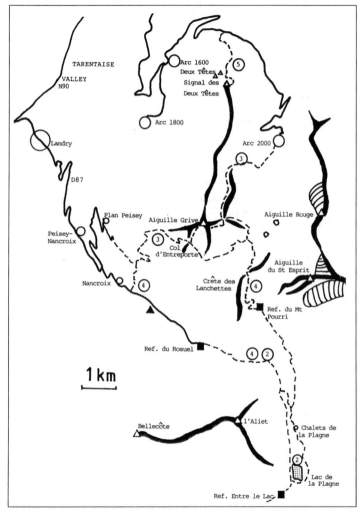

MAP 13. The Ponturin Valley and Les Arcs showing the lines taken by walk Nos. 2 to 5. A road (on Map 11) called the Chemin des Espagnols connects Arc 1800 with Plan Peisey

The Bellecôte in May, seen from the Balcon de Tarentaise. The sharp peak on its left is the Aliet (walk No. 4)

scree which requires care. The position is very impressive and it is not immediately evident exactly where the path is taking you. The path crosses to the foot of a wide grass slope near the Rousse and zig-zags up this to the Col d'Entreporte where you step across into very different, gentle country. Again, there are several paths and the one on the left leads to the summit of the Aiguille Grive. Note that the path straight ahead leads you round to the Arc 2000 ski area below the Col de la Chal.

Note: On certain days each week in the summer season, a chair-lift can be used from Plan Peisey which takes you above the forest line. This cuts out a lot of climbing, though it means missing Les Vernettes and the view towards the col you intend to cross.

From Arc 2000: The road goes through a tunnel under one of the buildings at Arc 2000 and on to garages with steps in front of you. The top of the steps opens out onto a large, flat area in front of an arcade with restaurants which is thronged in winter but very quiet in summer. On the far side is a track which climbs gently to a point where three sets of ski uplift start. Go right here and take the upper track which skirts around the end of a ridge, the Adret des Tuffes.

95

Once round the ridge, strike up onto its crest as soon as practicable and follow this towards the Aiguille Grive. Buildings housing ski uplift are encountered at the end of this ridge. Looking towards the Aiguille Grive, you can see a steep ridge rising to the left of its summit. Make for the foot of this and pick up the path which leads to the top, climbing directly at first, then traversing left near the crest of the summit ridge. This path is initially good but becomes a rather difficult surface of smooth, dry mud, steep and quite exposed near the top. You arrive on the south ridge of the mountain and follow this to the top.

Note: This approach may be blocked by a snow cornice early in the season and is not then practicable. It would be best to traverse around the mountain to the Col d'Entreporte and climb from there. The upper section of the path should be avoided in wet weather.

Descent: By either route. It is possible to walk to Arc 1800 or Arc 1600 from the open ground above Plan Peisey if you return via the Col d'Entreporte.

4: Refuge du Mt Pourri and Col d'Entreporte

Grade:	3
Map:	3532ET
Time needed:	6h 35min for circuit
Height gain:	1118m
Comment:	This is a circular walk in the upper part of the Peisey-Nancroix Valley which joins sections of Walks 2, 3 and 8 with some new ground. Horizontal distance 20km or 12¹/₂ miles

Approach: Drive to Rosuel as described for Walk No.2. It is possible to park a little lower down the valley, but go no lower than Pont Baudin.

Ascent: Follow the G.R.5 path from Rosuel towards the Lac de la Plagne as described for Walk No.2. Take the first path left in the upper valley and cross to another path which leads back on the left and climbs the flanks of Mt Pourri, making for the refuge of the same name. There are a couple of steep sections but otherwise the path is well graded. Refreshments can be obtained at the refuge. From

The Combe de la Neuva from La Terrasse
Young bouquetin feeding on one of the ridges of La Terrasse. The background is
the valley of Les Chapieux.

Le Crôt in autumn
Looking into Italy from the Col du Mont

there continue in the same direction on a path to the buildings at La Séviolière and climb on a green track which zig-zags up the hillside. Follow this up to the Crête des Lanchettes, which is the highest point of the day at 2548m, and continue towards the Col de la Chal. Another track will be seen below on the left and a path which leaves this near the chalets of the Plan des Eaux. Make for this path and follow it to the Col d'Entreporte (Walk No.3), cross the col and descend to the ski slopes of Plan Peisey. Turn left down through the woods and go past Notre Dame des Vernettes. A little below the chapel, a path leaves the track on the left and descends steeply to Pracompuet, then La Chénarie and the road, which is followed back to the car.

5: The Signal des Deux Têtes (2385m)

Grade:	2
Map:	3532ET
Time needed:	2h
Height gain:	590m
Comment:	The Deux Têtes are well known landmarks on the slopes of Les Arcs ski resort and are visible as you drive up the valley from Aime towards Bourg St Maurice as two little pinnacles of rock above and to the left of Arc 1600. Legend has it that they are the petrified remains of a man and a woman. The man had lost his wife and was living with another woman and his daughter. The two abused the daughter mercilessly until one day her boyfriend heard what was going on and his emotional reaction caused the powers of heaven and hell to rise against the couple and turn them to stone. The Signal is the summit just above the Deux Têtes

Approach: Drive from the valley in the direction of Arc 1600 and then Arc 2000. The road climbs quite quickly just after 1600 and there are two pronounced hairpin bends. The road then levels out and at an altitude marked as 1814m it is possible to park off the road. A good path leaves here and climbs through the forest. Alternatively, take the funicular from Bourg St Maurice to Arc 1600 and climb under the ski uplift until you reach a track which goes up to the left to a ski piste cleared through the forest. Follow a path there which meets up with the one first described.

Ascent: Continue through the opening in the forest until the foot of a ski tow is reached. From there a path climbs the steep slopes above in zig-zags and leads quite quickly to a wide track above the Deux Têtes whence they form an impressive foreground to the general view. To reach the Signal, follow this track up and round to the left until you are at the top of a chair-lift. On the right there is a wide, grassy gully which takes you quickly to the top.

Descent: By the same route or, better, via a little col to the south-east of the summit. Go right here and follow a steep track down, then around the base of the Signal towards the Deux Têtes.

6: Refuge de la Martin and Glacier de la Savinaz

Grade:	2
Map:	3532ET
Time needed:	2h 20min to glacier
Height gain:	540m
Comment:	An excellent path up the flanks of a big mountain takes the walker to the foot of a glacier and its moraine heaps. Good views to the hills on the frontier with Italy. La Gurraz, where the path starts, is itself worth a visit. It is an old village with traditional architecture and has benefited from a recent influx of younger people who work at the ski resorts. As a result, it manages to be both traditional and alive in a way that is very pleasing

Approach: If driving to Val d'Isère from St Foy, a fork right occurs a little before Les Pigettes which is signposted to Gurraz and Savine. Follow this road to the valley bottom and then climb the hillside on a narrow, twisting road, keeping straight on at the first junction and right at the second. There is a parking area just before you enter La Gurraz and a second through the village, at the start of the path.

Ascent: Keep to the upper track after the village and then follow the left-hand path which traverses at first and then climbs the hillside in zig-zags. Eventually, you cross the glacier torrent on a bridge; the white water is very impressive from this point. The path then climbs to the refuge whence several paths radiate. Two go south towards Les Brevières and the Vallon de la Sache while a third sets off northwest, crosses moraine and climbs to the foot of the glacier. It is possible to climb higher here and have a closer look at the séracs and ice walls of the higher part of the glacier. A path climbs more or less straight up the crest of the moraine heap to the left of the glacier to a point at about 2554m altitude. It is hard going, as are most climbs on moraine, but not difficult. It will take about an hour more than the time given above but provides good views both of the glacier and towards the mountains on the eastern side of the valley.

Descent: By the same route. It is also possible to descend to Les Brevières and return to La Savine and La Gurraz using a track which has been newly made along the valley.

7: La Gurraz to Villaroger via Refuge de Turia

Grade:	2
Map:	3532ET
Time needed:	5h 30min to Villaroger
Height gain:	818m
Comment:	A steep but good path takes you up to a refuge used by alpinists intent on climbing this side of Mont Pourri. The walk provides a contrast between the high mountain country and the mountain villages

Approach: Drive to La Gurraz as described for Walk No.6; also see the comment accompanying this walk.

Ascent: From the end of the road just behind the village, take the track which climbs steeply to the right. This becomes a path which mounts steadily with one or two respites and brings you to the refuge in little less than 2h. Traverse and descend into the combe beyond, cross the moraine and continue along the hillside below the

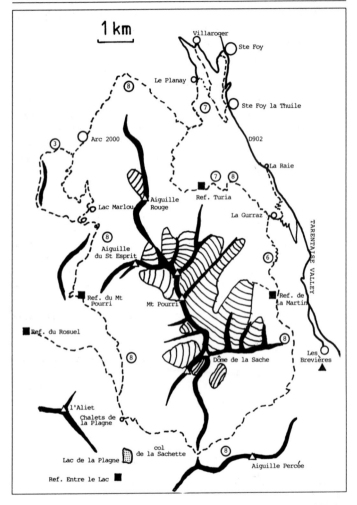

MAP 14. Mt Pourri and its glaciers. The lines of walk Nos. 6 and 7, the Tour of Mt Pourri (Walk 8) and a variation (3) are all shown. The lines of two short walks are included - La Raie to La Gurraz and the Villaroger circuit via Ste Foy

Aiguille Rouge. On your left as you leave the refuge is the gap of the Grand Col which allows access to the Les Arcs ski slopes. Above is Mont Turia which is a summit to the north of Mont Pourri and is connected to it by a sharp, graceful ridge. Continue to an altitude of about 1950m where there is a path which descends on the right. Follow this down through forest and clearings to the village of Le Planay from where a surfaced road takes you down to Le Pré and Villaroger. It will be evident from the map that this is not the only way to Le Planay and that there is a network of paths starting at the Plan de l'Aiguille which can be used to the same end, or to descend to the Auberge de Jeunesse near Longefoy - though I have not followed any of these myself.

Return to La Gurraz: This can be done on foot and will add about 2h to the day, as it involves some 475m ascent and some almost level sections. Go through Le Planay, and just as you emerge from the hamlet, turn right towards an electricity pylon and follow a poorly marked track which descends the fields below the houses. Continue down across the fields until you see a green track which traverses towards the buildings at Le Chapuis. Here you join a track which crosses a gully and then becomes a path which takes you to St Foy la Thuile. It is now necessary to walk up the road to La Raie. Just through the hamlet is a parking area on the right and beyond this, over the bridge, a track descends on the right. Follow this to the first bend, then take a path which continues up the valley to the Pont de la Gratte, across this and so up the old road to La Gurraz.

You do not, of course, need to be quite as energetic as this. If you have two cars leave one in a parking place near the river, below Villaroger, before going on to La Gurraz. If not, a taxi can be hired at the restaurant at Le Pré.

8: Tour of Mt Pourri

Grade:	2 with a very short section of 4
Map:	3532ET
Time needed:	About 2½ days with 2 nights in refuges
	At the moment only one of these, the Refuge du Mt Pourri, provides meals so provisions need to be carried

Comment: This is a tour of a big mountain following paths on its flanks. The terrain is varied and much is austere but magnificent

Approach: The tour can be started at Rosuel, La Gurraz or Arc 2000 and we will choose this last. Either drive from Bourg St Maurice up the Les Arcs road to Arc 2000, or use the funicular to Arc 1600 and the free *navette* (shuttle bus) to Arc 2000, though these may not be operating after early September.

First day: Arc 2000 to the Refuge du Mt Pourri

Time needed: 3h
Height gain: 600m

Set out as described for Walk No.3 but go straight on at the three sets of ski uplift on a track which follows the general line of the tows and climbs to Lac Marlou and to a smaller tarn which is reached shortly afterwards.

Alternative: Follow Walk No.3 as far as the ski uplift housing below the Aiguille Grive and follow the track to the left to the Col de la Chal and the second tarn. This adds about 100m of ascent but avoids much of the ski uplift.

From the lake take a not too well defined path in the direction of the Grand Col. This climbs a shallow scree gully and then goes sharp right over a rocky terrace near the top of some rocks to bring you almost immediately to the Lac des Moutons, a quite idyllic place. The path, which is now well marked and remains so, takes a gently descending sweep around the combe ahead, below the Crête des Lanchettes to the refuge which can soon be seen below. Follow either the marked path or a green track which crosses the valley behind the refuge.

Second day: Refuge du Mt Pourri to Refuge de la Martin

Time needed: 5h 30min
Height gain: 790m in three stages

Take the path which descends from the refuge, heading towards the Lac de la Plagne. This traverses below the rocks of Mt Pourri, descending in a couple of steps until you are on the level, upper part of the Ponturin Valley. Continue to the Chalets de la Plagne where a path goes off left and tackles immediately the steep slopes ahead.

Height is gained quickly until you enter an upper valley, the Plan de la Sache, surrounded by ridges bristling with odd shaped pinnacles. The Col de la Sachette, which is the day's highest point, is visible high on the right. The path swings around the bowl of the valley and climbs through rocky chaos to the col.

The first few metres of descent from the col provide the only real difficulty of the whole tour. Two paths will be seen going off to the left. The upper one leads to a little gully which can be used to descend to the path. The lower leads to a traverse of a few metres around an exposed corner which, if approached from below, appears to be the main route. This provides a few moments of excitement. A good path now traverses and descends steep slopes until gentler ground is reached, which holds several little tarns. The scenery remains very rocky and the tongue of the Glacier Suspendu, below the Dôme de la Sache, may jettison some ice onto the Glacier Plan below. Descend to the Chalet de la Sache d'en Haut where the path crosses a track and passes close by the chalet. A steep descent follows to a bridge across the Ruisseau de la Sachette. From now on the views are across the trough of the upper Tarentaise Valley. The path crosses open slopes with a couple of sustained ascents to arrive at the Refuge de la Martin. As described for Walk No.6, you should walk up to the Glacier de la Savinaz after you are installed in the refuge. It is a feature of this tour that while the views across the valley are always splendid, the glaciers of Mt Pourri itself are almost all hidden by the rock buttresses which support them, and this short climb is the best way to approach close to one.

Third day: Refuge de la Martin to Arc 2000

Time needed: 6h 30min
Height gain: 980m

Descend to La Gurraz as described for Walk No.6 and continue along the track which leads to the Refuge de Turia as described for Walk No.7 and on towards Le Planay. At the junction near Le Crêt, where a path descends to Le Planay, continue left around a steep little ravine where the path is rather narrow, then over open slopes to a second path junction where it is possible to descend to Plan de l'Aiguille. Again keep left. Along this section of the tour, Mt Blanc is always visible ahead and the Tête du Rutor across the valley. The twin glaciers of les Balmes are also there but you have to look back to see these. The path climbs gently until it reaches a track, part of the ski resort of Villaroger. Climb the track, steeply at first, to and past the chair-lift of the Plan des Violettes. At the next sharp left-hand bend a path climbs a small bank and traverses rocky slopes clothed with Arolla pine, whose seeds are the favoured food of the bird known as the nutcracker, which you may see here. The area has also been made a reserve for the attractive gallinacious bird known in France as the tetras lyre and as the black grouse in the UK. This bird is present in quite large numbers in the National Park but finds it difficult to co-exist with ski resorts, and here you see an attempt to preserve it near Les Arcs. The buildings of Arc 2000 soon come into view, the path descends to a track and the loop of the walk is nearly complete.

Summary of refuges

Du Mt Pourri - Altitude 2370m. Meals provided. 56 beds (79 07 90 43 for booking). Club Alpin Français.

De la Martin - Altitude 2154m. 34 beds (79 06 44 32). Parc National de la Vanoise. This refuge may soon be extended and provide meals from 1995 - but check first.

De Turia - Altitude 2428m. 24 beds. Parc National de la Vanoise.

SOME SHORT WALKS

Villaroger-La Thuile - Drive to Ste Foy Tarentaise and take the road signposted to Villaroger. Cross the Isère and climb a little to where there is a large parking place on the right for your car. Continue on foot up the road to Villaroger and climb through the village to the point where you are about to enter a large square. Just on the left, a road goes up to the left and joins a surfaced road which climbs steeply to Le Pré, being an alternative to the normal motor road which goes to the right after the square. At the hairpin bend an obvious track goes off on the left and climbs gradually through open forest and past some impressive waterfalls to the chalets known as Le Chapuis. Here, the track becomes a path and continues into and round a steep gully, which in winter and spring is full of avalanche snow fallen from the slopes of the Aiguille Rouge above. The path continues through forest and under an enormous overhanging rock and soon after reaches open fields and a pleasant place for a picnic.

Take the bridge across the Isère and climb easily to La Thuile on a good track. A moment before this reaches the main road, there is a little surfaced road which descends on the left and quickly turns into a good path which allows you to avoid the main road while running parallel with it. The path descends to a building used for dances and with a pair of football goal posts outside. Walk to the main road where you will see a small concrete wall on the left. At its nearest end, a well concealed set of steps descends below the level of the road and leads to a path to the hamlet of Le Jorat. Here, two paths go off to the left, one in front of a farm and a second almost immediately after, which is the one to take. As you approach Ste Foy the path widens and a second path descends on the left. It is preferable to take this as it completely avoids the main road. It leads between some houses and then a green track will be seen descending steeply to the left and which leads directly to the Villaroger road and so to the car park. - *Grade 1.* This is a round trip which is likely to take about 1h 40min.

La Raie-La Gurraz - There is a large parking area just to the south of La Raie, which is a hamlet on the main road between Ste Foy and Val d'Isère. A few paces in the direction of Val, across a bridge, a rough track descends to the river and to a bridge at Covier. At the first bend, a wide path continues along the valley. This is straightforward at first but becomes somewhat overgrown later, though always passable. It joins a green track descending on the left and this leads quickly to a graceful stone arched bridge across the Isère with an attractive waterfall just upriver. This is the Pont de la Gratte. The cliffs across the river look impracticable, but an excellent way has in the past been made through them and leads without difficulty to the modern road to La Gurraz. This should be followed to the village, which is well worth visiting for its last century charm - a charm augmented by the fact that it is still an inhabited settlement. Return to the car necessarily by the same route. Allow 1hr 10min there, 50min to return. - *Grade 2.*

The Croix de Montrigon - This is a steepish walk on the north-facing, forested slopes below Les Arcs. A glance at the map will show that this hillside from Villaroger round to Landry is seamed with marked footpaths which can be organised into a variety of day outings. The one described is typical in many ways of these walks - the shade of the woods, the villages and churches, and easy accessibility from valley or ski resort. In the present case there is in addition a rather splendid cross to be seen, placed by an old mule track to remind peasants in times past that His toils were greater than theirs. The cross at Montrigon is decorated with carvings of the objects involved in the Passion. We describe here the ascent up the old track to get you in the right frame of mind, but it is also possible to drive to the spot, if you prefer.

The walk starts near Bourg St Maurice, from the bridge over the Isère river near the car park for the funicular. Park here or near the bridge. Cross the river and immediately take a path up the hillside signposted to Notre Dame de Tout Pouvoir. The path goes more or less straight up, passing the chapel on wooden steps. Cross the main Les Arcs road and then a minor road, which is ascended for a short way before continuing up a path to the cross itself. Now walk up through the village of Montrigon and go right, then left, straight up to the main road again. This last short section is very steep but can be avoided by faint zig-zags on the right. The next section is uncompromisingly steep. The path goes straight up the hillside in a well worn trough from which one escapes to the right on a path which goes to the side and brings you to a good path which comes up on the right. This starts from the western end of Montrigon and would probably make a much less fatiguing approach, though not recommended in the local maps. Follow the new path to the left, traversing onto open field and around an isolated chalet. Aim now for the left-hand house of Les Granges which you pass on its right and continue straight up over the fields to the hamlet of L'Orgière. From here the path continues up some steps in the direction of Les Arcs but you need to go left on a green track which leads to a minor, surfaced road.

Up to this point the way has been shown by yellow markers which, from this point on, become much more useful. Follow the road up until a track goes down on the left, just before a hairpin bend. An L-shaped arrow directs you to a good path which descends in zig-zags and brings you in sight of two large water conduits. These feed the turbines of the Malgovert power station below with water which has been brought in tunnels under Mont Pourri from near Les Brevières below the Barrage at Tignes. The path touches the road and then continues in zig-zags through the forest to meet the road a second time. Follow this, taking the turning to Montrigon and then a path to the right at a small post. Reach and cross a track then continue, going right at the first fork and left at the second. This brings you out on the main road which is ascended a little to the junction with the road down to Bourg and the car. Allow 2h 40min for the round trip. This walk is capable of almost infinite variation, as a glance at the map will show. These walks are steep in places. - *Grade 2.*

Notre Dame des Vernettes - This walk is described as part of Walk No.3, starting at Plan Peisey, and is well worth doing. There are plenty of places to picnic and magnificent views across the valley to the Bellecôte. It is possible to continue by following an obvious path which climbs to the left and take a branch which contours through the woods and eventually allows a descent to be made to the starting point. This part of the route is not marked on the map but should present no difficulty. Allow 50min to the church. - *Grade 1.*

Cascade du Py - Drive from Moûtiers via Bozel to Champagny and from there take the exciting narrow little road to Champagny le Haut. The exposed part of this road is narrow but is well guarded and leads to a high valley with several attractive hamlets and with views of the Grande Motte at the head of the valley. The road ends at Le Laissonay where there is parking. The waterfall will be obvious from here, up to the left, and can be approached on a good path, which leads to the Refuge de Plaisance. There is also parking at Le Bois, lower down the valley, and a pleasant walk is to be had between there and Le Laisonnay. Allow 1h 20min to the top of the waterfall. - *Grade 1* in the valley; *Grade 2* to the top of the waterfall.

Lac des Moutons has already been described in Walk No.8, first day. It can be reached, as described, from Arc 1800 using the Transarc cable-car (if operating) and following the track which descends in the direction of the Col de la Chal.

CHAPTER 4:
The Beaufortain and Northern Tarentaise

INTRODUCTION

This region extends from Albertville in the west to the valley of Les Chapieux, north of Bourg St Maurice. The hills form the watershed between the Tarentaise and Beaufortain valleys. The cirque of the latter is completed by a ridge to the north, which separates it from the Megève area, and another ridge which is effectively the western tail of the Mt Blanc range. The town of Beaufort is reached by road from Albertville, and there is also access by three high cols: the Col des Saisies from Megève, the Cormet de Roselend from Bourg St Maurice (cormet is a local word for col), and the mostly unsurfaced Cormet d'Arêches from Aime. There is also the Col Joly, which can be reached from Beaufort by car but not crossed, and which is a walkers' way over to Les Contamines de Montjoie. The Beaufortain is a pastoral valley which in places is reminiscent of the Swiss Alps, particularly around the village of Arêches. There are also several artificial lakes, part of the hydro-electric system, pleasantly situated among the hills, the largest being the Barrage de Roselend.

The walking here is very varied; parts are reminiscent of Scotland while elsewhere it is decidedly alpine, though the region has no glaciers, a lack which is compensated by the proximity of the snows of Mt Blanc which can be seen from almost all high points. To the north it is usually possible to see the long limestone ridge of the Massif des Aravis, which makes an imposing horizon, while to the south, from the watershed with the Tarentaise, the bigger mountains of Vanoise and Tarentaise make a magnificent vista. There are several walkers' ways over from Tarentaise to Beaufortain so that it is quite possible to make short circular tours, and the long-distance walk known as "the Tour of the Beaufortain" gives an overall view of the whole region. Looking north from the trough of the Tarentaise Valley it is difficult to realise the extent of the hill country lying between you and the Beaufortain, since this is hidden by the valley sides. A number of tributary valleys penetrate deeply into the hills and it is only from the upper reaches of these that a true idea of the

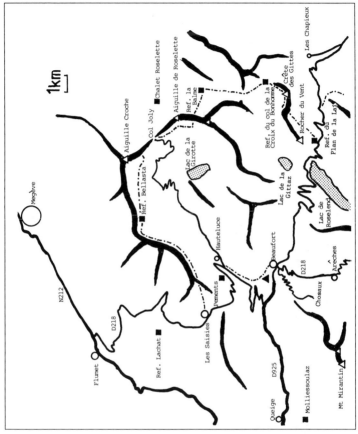

MAP 15. The northern half of the region described in Chapter 4 including most of the Beaufortain. Main features and access roads are shown together with the route of the Tour du Beaufortain described. The locations of the refuges are also shown

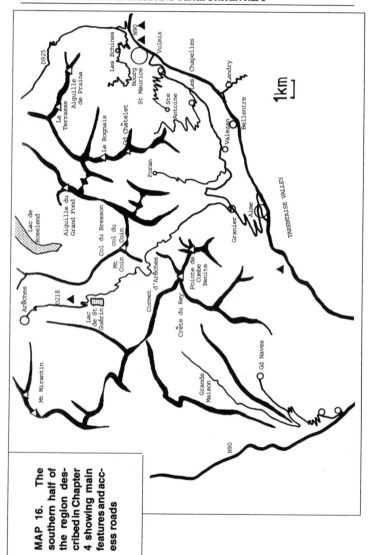

MAP 16. The southern half of the region described in Chapter 4 showing main features and access roads

Heading for Mt Mirantin (walk 1)

magnificence of the scenery can be obtained.

The weather in the Beaufortain requires some additional comment. Possibly because it is the furthest north we go, or because of the proximity of enormous Mt Blanc, the weather is less stable than in the Tarentaise. Thunderstorms may rage over Roselend while Bourg St Maurice basks in sunshine. It is thus essential when walking in this part of the region to pay particular attention to the weather forecasts.

The area described is covered completely by the 1:50,000 R&D map "Mt Blanc and Beaufortain" but two maps are needed at the 1:25,000 scale: TOP25 series 3532OT "Massif du Beaufortain" (which covers most of the walking) and 3531OT "Megève" which is needed for the northern half of the tour of the Beaufortain. Even then, a small region to the east is omitted and map 3532ET "Les Arcs. La Plagne" is needed for the Aiguille de Praina.

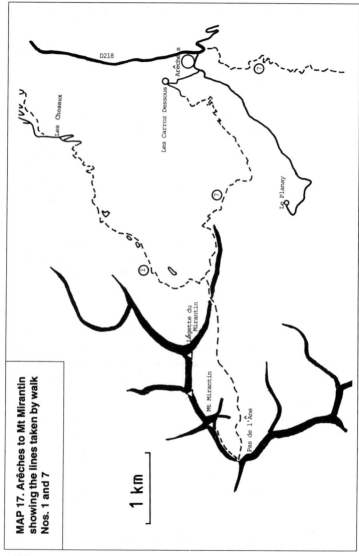

MAP 17. Arêches to Mt Mirantin showing the lines taken by walk Nos. 1 and 7

D218

Les Choseaux

Arêches

Les Carroz Dessous

Le Planay

Légette du Mirantin

Mt Mirantin

Pas de l'Âne

1 km

1: Pas de l'Âne and Mt Mirantin (2460m)

Grade:	3 to Pas, 4 to summit, but only a short section at this grade
Map:	3532OT
Time needed:	3h 50min
Height gain:	1160m
Comment:	Mt Mirantin is visible from Albertville and is one of the guardians of the entrance to the Beaufortain Valley. A superb view is obtained of the Combe de Savoie, 2100m, below and this gives the mountain stature greater than its height would suggest. It also has several shapely and impressive neighbour peaks. As a day outing, it is best approached from Beaufort or Arêches

Approach: From Beaufort, take the turning for Arêches but immediately after crossing the river, take a road right which climbs the hillside to the south-west in a series of zig-zags. A left turn leads to Les Chosaux and you should park a little higher on open hillside, at about 1300m altitude. The ascent will be described from here. If starting from Arêches it is possible to drive to Le Planay.

Ascent: A path climbs more or less straight up the hillside ahead and passes three small tarns in turn. The first is marked Le Clou in black and the third Lac Couvert in blue. In fact, the paths here are somewhat confusing on the ground, particularly in the forest, and map and compass will be useful, if not essential. You emerge onto open hillside in a little valley with the Légette du Mirantin at its head. Follow this on gently sloping ground until rocks virtually force you to climb a steep slope on the left onto a ridge. Here, you join a good path (Tour du Beaufortain) where you go right and traverse above the steep head of a second valley. This leads without difficulty to the Pas de l'Âne. The ridge on your right leads to Mt Mirantin, which is only a short ascent from here, but with a little wall in its central part which requires use of the hands to pass.

Descent: By the same route. The map suggests many possible variations to the route but the one described, with its little tarns, is the prettiest.

The Légette de Mirantin with Mt Blanc in the distance

2: The Lacs de la Tempête via Col de la Louze (2119m)

Grade:	2
Map:	3532OT
Time needed:	2h
Height gain:	500m
Comment:	This is an outing which almost qualifies as a "short walk" except that it goes quite high. The tarns lie in a pretty little valley with much of the alpine scenery hidden from view and this, plus the nature of the terrain, makes for a corner of the region which is very evocative of the Scottish hills

Approach: If driving, turn off the N90 expressway at Aigueblanche and take the road to Grand Coeur, then Petit Coeur (D93) from where the road zig-zags up the steep side of a ridge, then heads in the direction of Grand Naves. At the fourth hairpin bend above the village of Molencon (alt. 1111m) take a track left which quickly enters the forest, then traverses around the end of a ridge in an impressively exposed position and enters the Vallée de la Grande Maison. This is a long, straight, V-shaped valley and is heavily forested. The track continues for 9km and is rough but adequate. Parking at 1629m. Alternatively, if staying in the Beaufortain, drive to and park at the Lac de St Guérin (1559m).

Ascent: Follow the path (marked Tour du Beaufortain) to the Col de la Louze. From the col take a path which descends to the west and reaches the Lacs de la Tempête in a few minutes.

Descent: By the same route.

3: Cormet d'Arêches and Mt Coin (2539m)

Grade:	2
Map:	3532OT
Time needed:	For ascent - 1h 40min from Cormet d'Arêches or 2h from Plan Pichu
Comment:	A simple ascent among pleasant scenery terminating in a narrow summit ridge

Approach: The Cormet d'Arêches is the highest point on the road linking the village of Granier in the Tarentaise with that of Arêches in the Beaufortain. The road is surfaced from Granier to just after the hamlet of Laval and from Arêches to Lac St Guérin. In between is a rough track which is passable to any vehicle with adequate ground clearance, though there is an awkward stream ford just after Plan Pichu on the Granier side which will stop some cars. From here, one can walk either up the road to the cormet or take an obvious track on the opposite side of the valley. Several walks pass over or near the cormet and there is a refuge just below the summit on the Granier side (Refuge de la Coire - see Walk No.4 for details). This has a guardian and provides refreshments. There is ample parking on the cormet itself and an excellent picnic spot, the Lac des Fées, on the Arêches side at an altitude of 1896m.

Ascent: If made from the refuge, take a track which forks left off the cormet track just below the refuge, ie. set out towards Laval. Go left again immediately before an isolated chalet and climb to a level bottomed combe. If starting from the cormet, take an obvious path which goes north-east and follows a ridge towards a great, wooden cross called the Croix du Berger. Continue past this through little canyons with a rocky chaos to the left and pinnacles overhanging the Lac des Fées below. Climb a little and then go right, across to the level bottom of the combe just mentioned, for the start from the refuge. Continue towards a ridge which leads to the summit. An adequate path climbs the side of this ridge and then follows it to the summit. This is quite a narrow crest, but with places to picnic and splendid views of the Crête du Rey and the Combe Bénite beyond the cormet, while to the east, Mt Blanc forms a backdrop to rocky summits, the most notable of which is the pillar of the Pierra Menta, a rock climber's peak which was first climbed as recently as 1925.

Descent: By the same route, except that the path to the cormet is so pretty that anyone starting from the refuge is advised to return via the Croix du Berger.

4: Crête du Rey (2633m)

Grade:	4
Map:	3532OT
Time needed:	1h 50min from Cormet d'Arêches, about the same for the descent. It is possible to start from a lower altitude, when suitable additional time should be allowed
Comment:	This is an isolated peak with a very steep approach to the summit and an airy ridge traverse. It is a well worthwhile ascent, though short. We will describe a circuit involving the traverse of the summit ridge

Approach: By car over surfaced road, then rough track from either Aime or Arêches to the summit of the Cormet d'Arêches where there is ample parking. The Refuge de la Coire (pronounced "kwar") is just below the summit of the col on its south side and is a good starting point for the non-motorised walker.

Ascent: From the cormet the peak is slightly west of south. A ridge falls steeply to the left of the summit to a shoulder where it divides

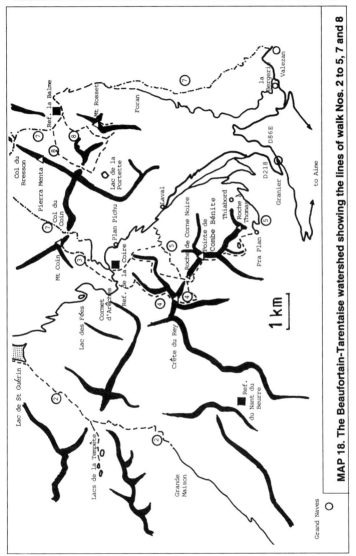

MAP 18. The Beaufortain-Tarentaise watershed showing the lines of walk Nos. 2 to 5, 7 and 8

The Crête du Rey from the Croix du Berger

into two, the ridge nearest to you hiding the other. While no path is marked on the map, an adequate path climbs up the face of this ridge to its crest below the shoulder. Set out south along a good track, marked "Tour du Beaufortain" on the TOP25 map, but quickly strike right towards the ridge over grassy slopes, pivoting around an old rain gauge. Traverse around a slight hollow to the foot of the screes and pick up a path which takes a rising traverse left and then turns right to follow the line of the ridge. The path keeps below the crest of the ridge, on its right. Eventually, easier ground and then the shoulder are reached. (Note that it is equally possible to follow the "Tour" path to a point marked 2313m and then follow the second ridge. This is easier and makes a pleasant return route for anyone not wishing to make the traverse of the peak.)

From the shoulder the path continues straight up and hands are needed at times. The angle eases off momentarily half-way up but the route climbs steeply again towards the top of an open and exposed gully. It is not, however, necessary to cross this, you can avoid it by a short scramble on the left. The summit is reached abruptly and then a few exposed steps across the top of the gully lead to a wide grassy platform made for picnics. A scree gully descends from here into the combe south of the peak and is said to provide a quick way down if caught by bad weather. Your route continues along the crest of the mountain until a boss on the right indicates that you should now tend left, on a trace of a path which descends towards a ridge leading south. This part is exposed above steep grass slopes and is probably best avoided in wet conditions. You are quickly on the ridge itself, which provides easy ground leading to an obvious col from where a herdsman's path traverses back to the left into the southern combe of the mountain and onto its floor, which provides very pleasant walking in the direction of the Roche de Corne Noire. This feature is neither rocky nor black from this side but has the form of a green cone. The col of the same name is on its left and the ridge is crossed here. A short climb leads to the col and a path descends quite steeply into and then traverses the combe beyond to join the "Tour" path which is followed back to the Cormet d'Arêches.

Alternatives: The peak could equally be approached via Grand Naves and the Refuge du Nant du Beurre and crossing the Col de la Grande Combe. It could also be combined with Walk No.5, though this would only be possible for a strong party.

Since the walk is relatively short, even if difficult, there may be time to climb the Crête du Boeuf also. This poses no difficulties and carries an abundant flora in early summer.

Summary of refuges

De la Coire - Altitude 2060m. Meals provided. Open mid June to end September. Up to 40 beds (79 09 70 92 for information and booking - the 'phone uses a radio link which is sometimes poor). Owned by the commune of Granier.

Du Nant du Beurre - Altitude 2100m. No guardian, keys at Restaurant Belleview, Grande Naves (79 24 01 31). 30 beds. Owned by the commune of La Léchère.

5: Pointe de Combe Bénite (2575m)

Grade:	3
Map:	3532OT
Time needed:	For ascent 3h 25min from from Laval. Descent will take about 2h
Height gain:	875m
Comment:	We describe a circuit involving a traverse of the whole mountain. This is much more rounded than the Crête du Rey though the descent from the summit follows a sharp and airy ridge. Sheep may be encountered near the top, which may bring back memories of home!

Approach: From Aime take the road through Tessens and Granier. Climb through the village and follow the road to the Cormet d'Arêches as far as the hamlet of Laval, where the car can be parked. For those without transport, the Refuge de la Coire can be used as either starting point or finish.

Ascent: The road crosses the river at Laval and immediately after the bridge, a track starts on the left, returning down the valley. Follow this to a fork (1622m) and take the right-hand track up through the forest. This meets another track at a hairpin where you go right and continue to climb, aiming for a point at 1979m near the hamlet of La Traversaz. Though the track is marked as ending here, it in fact continues, climbing only slowly towards the hamlet of Pra Plan. The rocks of the Roche à Thomas will be observed ahead and later on the right as the hamlet is approached.

About 200m before the hamlet, leave the track and climb right up a grassy hollow making for a col below and to the left of Roche à Thomas. There is no path at first but if you tend to the left one will be picked up to take you to the col without difficulty. Cross the col and walk past the strangely dirty Lac de Guio. The easiest way from here is to pass the lake and climb onto a subsidiary ridge behind, which is in fact little more than a fold in the terrain, and which takes you north-east to meet the ridge which connects the point, 2513m, with the Roche à Thomas. A path is encountered here, which

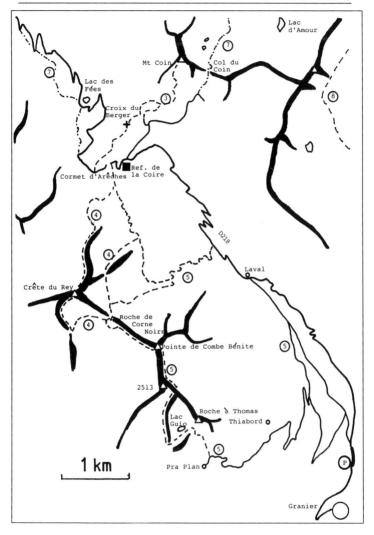

Map 19. The central part of Map 18 showing some of the walks in a little more detail. The 'P' indicates the parking area above Granier

suggests that many climb directly from the col before the lake, directly onto this ridge. Continue left and pass the point at 2513m to arrive quickly at the Pointe de Combe Bénite. This is an excellent viewpoint for the Tarentaise hills. A particular feature is the dolomite-like monolith of the Pierra Menta visible to the north-east.

Descent: The same route as the ascent may be used but it is much better to continue and make a circuit. From just past the summit a sharp ridge can be seen which descends in the direction of the Crête du Rey with steep grass slopes on the left and rock and scree on its right. The crest of this ridge can be followed without great difficulty, though here and there care is needed. There is a trace of a path, though the way seems to be little used. The scree gullies on the right are home to an abundant population of the honey scented *Thlaspi rotundifolium*.

Follow the ridge to a little before the green cone of the Roche de Corne Noire and descend steep grass on the left at any convenient point to gain a good path which climbs from below. Follow this around the cone, climb to the Col de Corne Noire and descend the track into the combe beyond. About a third of the way across the combe, leave the path and descend towards the bottom of the combe, making for a grassy barrier to the left of the stream where this disappears over an edge. Go left along the top of the barrier and look for a path which descends its steep outer face. At the foot of the slope the path enters a boulder field where it is difficult to pick a way. Keep left and make for the good path marked "Tour du Beaufortain" on the TOP25 map. Go right and follow the path down to the road near Laval.

Alternatives: If using the Refuge de la Coire, the last combe has to be crossed entirely and the "Tour" path joined at much higher altitude. A long, more energetic circuit can be made by parking at a wide parking area above Granier, by a ski tow, at an altitude of 1410m. Follow the track up through the forest, going left then right, to meet the route already described. Allow 8h for this variation.

6: Rocher du Vent and Crête des Gittes (2380m and 2358m respectively)

Grade:	2
Maps:	The area in question is right on the join between maps 3532OT and 3531OT. There is some overlap but, confusingly, the footpaths marked red are not the same on the two maps. Note also that the Crête des Gittes path is part of the Tour of the Beaufortain and is on the long-distance path G.R.5
Time needed:	For ascent Les Chapieux-Crête-Rocher-La Lai will take 5h 20min, the reverse a little less. If starting from the cormet, allow 4h. If doing the full circuit on foot, allow 1h 20min from La Lai to the cormet and about 1h down to Les Chapieux
Comment:	The mountains in question form the hillside to the north of the Cormet de Roselend with three possible starting points: Plan de la Lai, the cormet itself, or Les Chapieux. It is a region to explore at will, visiting either or both named summits - the impressive ridge of the Crête or the curious Rocher, whose summit is in fact a little open-ended valley between two blades of rock. We will describe a circuit taking in both title features

Approach: By road from either Beaufort or Bourg St Maurice on the Cormet de Roselend road. There are refuges at Plan de la Lai and at Les Chapieux (Refuge de la Nova). There is also one near the north-eastern end of the Crête, Refuge du Col de la Croix du Bonhomme, which is used both on the Tour of the Beaufortain and the Tour of Mt Blanc.

The circuit described can be done in either direction.

Ascent: From the road just through the hamlet of Les Chapieux take the footpath north which zig-zags up steep ground to the Refuge du Col de la Croix du Bonhomme (refreshments). At the refuge go left, making for the sharp and impressive ridge ahead which is the Crête des Gittes seen end-on. The traverse of this ridge is much easier than

The Rocher du Vent. The hidden canyon lies behind the near blade of rock

it appears from a distance and is along a broad path cut into the steep northern slope. If the path is blocked by snow, it is preferable to cross to the grassy southern side. The end of the ridge is reached without difficulty, the path drops to the Col de la Sauce and descends gently at first towards the Plan de la Lai. Some 500m from the col, a poor path traverses horizontally across steep grass towards the Rocher du Vent, passing a small wrecked aircraft on the way, eventually reaching a better path onto the ridge which arrives at the entrance to this strange elevated "valleylet" or canyon. Walk to the end for a magnificent sight with the Barrage de Roselend apparently at your feet and 800m below. An alternative, which involves losing a little more height, is to descend to the chalet at Bel Air, traverse to La Lauze and follow the path as before.

Descent: By the path from the entrance to the canyon down to Plan de la Lai.

The Tunnel: For some unaccountable reason, someone has pierced a tunnel through the western end of the southern summit rock blade. Up to now, I have not been able to find anyone who knows its purpose. It is said to be possible to walk through this tunnel and arrive on a steep slope below the far end of the canyon.

Alternatives: From the Cormet de Roselend, follow an obvious track which goes north from the eastern end of the car park. After about 1km it is possible to pick a route up the grassy slopes ahead, following one of several alternatives, and arrive on the Crête des Gittes. These slopes carry an abundant flora, particularly in July.

Summary of refuges

Plan de la Lai - Altitude 1816m. Meals provide., 30 beds (79 38 90 82 for information and booking). Club Alpin Français.

Refuge de la Nova - Altitude 1550m. Meals provided. 41 beds (79 07 00 36 for information and booking). Private.

7: The Tour of the Beaufortain

Grade: 2 with short passages of 3
Time needed: This is a long tour and needs 8 or 9 days. The stages described do not have to be adhered to, particularly for the latter half of the tour where there is plenty of alternative accommodation, and some flexibility has been included in the descriptions

Introduction: The Tour of the Beaufortain is a very variable feast. I possess two publications which contain different routes and the 1990 D&R guide (see booklist in introduction) gives a much longer version with many of the earlier used sections given as variations, the menu being very much à la carte. The corresponding routes are marked on the new TOP25 maps 3531OT and 3532OT which are needed to cover the whole area traversed. The tour passes through some very pleasant countryside and has the added attraction that it is much quieter than the neighbouring Tour of Mt Blanc, as you will find on the short section where the two coincide.

I will give a version that we did in 1980, though the accommodation has changed so much around Beaufort that I will be forced to describe bits that I have not been able to check. I have discovered that some accommodation marked on the maps no longer exists and that much other, non-marked, accommodation does exist. Up-to-date information on lodging can be obtained from the tourist office at Beaufort (79 38 37 57) and the D&R guide is also useful. My purpose is simply to point out the possible delights of this walk and show how it liaises with the walks of the Tarentaise.

Approach: Starting and finishing points can be almost anywhere on a circular tour and Queige, to the west of Beaufort, is the "official" starting point, though this involves using a long section in forest, which my personal prejudices will lead me to avoid. For the car-less visitor from the UK it is probably least trouble to travel to Bourg St Maurice which has a good train service, and start from Landry station.

Alternatively, you could start at Les Contamines de Montjoie which is situated not far from Chamonix.

First day: Valezan to La Balme

Time needed: From Valezan 3h 10min, 5h 10min from Landry station

The route follows the G.R.5 long-distance path. Walk up to Landry from the station and at the crossroads (by a bridge), turn right and follow a road (D220) along the bottom of the valley. Turn right at the next bridge and cross the Isère to Bellentre whence the path climbs to Valezan. This point can be reached by taxi from Aime or Bourg if time so dictates. Climb directly up through the village and make a rising traverse across open hillside with views of old, pastoral villages, until the path takes you into the valley of the Ormente torrent with the rock slabs of the Pointe de Gargan ahead. The valley is known after a chalet called Foran, which can be reached by road as described in Walk No.8, and makes a convenient starting point for anyone with transport. The path continues up the valley and eventually joins the track from Foran where it crosses a bridge. This now leads directly to the Refuge Communal de la Balme with food and accommodation.

Second day: La Balme to the Refuge de la Coire

Time needed: 5h 15min, total ascent 898m. The first two days could be combined by a fit party starting from Foran, but 8h 45min are needed and the total ascent becomes 1267m

Set off behind the refuge and follow the path to the right around the hillside into a little valley. The Refuge de Presset is up on the right and this provides alternative accommodation, though there is no guardian. The path swings left and climbs slopes to the Col de Bresson (2469m). Cross the col and descend to the chalet, also called Presset on the map, where a minor path goes off to the left into a valley leading south-west. The path swings across the stream and up to the chalets at Conchette and then makes a bee-line for the Col du Coin. Mt Coin is visible on the right (Walk No.3) and the Pierra Menta is above on the left, this striking column remaining in view for much of the first two days. The climb up the final steep slopes to the col counts as one of the grade 3 passages as the path traverses left across the upper slopes on outward-sloping scree and can be quite awkward. Two little tarns can be seen to the north, nestled in the bottom of a combe, which attract picnickers. It is not possible to reach Mt Coin from here as the connecting ridge is blocked by a rock pinnacle. A narrow path descends steep grass from the col and quickly joins a track which leads directly to the Refuge de la Coire. To reach Mt Coin either take the track off right, as described for Walk No.3, or climb easy grass slopes to a pond which can be seen on the right from the col and follow a path which traverses from there to join the path up the ridge.

Third day: From la Coire to Arêches

Time needed: 5h 20min
Height gain/loss: Ascent 476m, descent 1580m

Climb the short distance to the Cormet d'Arêches and then make for Arêches itself, either by the track or by a steeper path which cuts out some of the meanderings of the track. Both routes pass the pretty Lac des Fées, and both end on the dam of the Lac de St Guérin. This lake always looks unbelievably blue from above and it is hard to realise that it is man-made when looking down on it from the hills. Arêches lies at the foot of the valley but the tour follows high ground on one side or the other. My original route took paths on the eastern side of the valley but these proved difficult to find and it seems to me better to follow the route marked on the TOP25 map. Thus, walk up the western shore of the lake on a track and take a path which rises steeply through the forest and which passes near the Tête de Cuvy (1991m) and then descends to Arêches. There are hotels here and a refuge, la Grangette.

Note: There is an alternative to day 3 and day 4 which may be preferable and keeps you higher. Climb towards the Tête de Cuvy but take a path on the left which traverses the slopes of the Grand Mont to the Refuge des Arolles which can be used as a stopping place (79 38 12 63, meals provided).

From les Arolles climb a little and then descend to the Col de la Bathie from where a path (red and yellow waymarks) traverses to the left, crosses a stream and then splits, at which point you take the left fork and climb steeply for a while. The path then follows the Lavouet stream, almost to the tarn of the same name, and strikes uphill again, now on pathless ground, making for the Col des Lacs. This and the next section are marked as difficult on the map but in fact present no problems. You arrive at the col to find the way barred by a steep drop. Go right and climb a little until the path takes you over onto less steep ground and traverses to below the Pas de l'Âne. Proceed to Beaufort or Queige, as desired.

I have not yet been able to survey the whole of this variation but can at least assure you not to worry about the section marked with dots on the map.

Fourth day: Beaufort via the Pas de l'Âne and Mt Mirantin

Time needed: Allow 8h 40min from Arêches to Beaufort or 11h 20min if you intend to go as far as the Gîte d'Étape at Pemonts. This is a long day and it is essential to reserve accommodation ahead to avoid disappointment. Much of the route has already been given in Walk No.1

Follow the "Tour du Beaufortain" path from Arêches via Les Carroz Dessous through the forest to Plan Villard and soon after onto open hillside. The path leads directly to the Pas de l'Âne, joining quite quickly the route of Walk No.1. Caching the rucksacks near here could make sense. Make the ascent of Mt Mirantin, if desired. Return in the direction of the ascent but descend left, into a small valley east of the Légette du Mirantin and make for Lac

On the slopes of the Acheboc with the Pointe de l'Argentière behind and
Lac Blanc below

Couvert, Le Clou and then Les Chosaux. A path descends below the hamlet and allows you to miss out almost all of the road down to Beaufort where there are hotels. Les Pemonts is reached by taking a path which starts near the swimming pool, climbs using a short section of road and then makes in the direction of Hauteluce. When the road is reached again, follow this to Pemonts.

The "official" tour takes you across the Pas de l'Âne and descends to a gîte at Molliesoulaz. This gives a shorter stage but involves a lot of walking in forest and takes you as low as 540m altitude.

Fifth day: Les Pements to Refuge de la Balme

Time needed: This is a long day which, following the previous long section, may be better to shorten. Fortunately, there is accommodation available along the way. Allow 4h to the Col de Véry, 5h 20min to the Col Joly and 7h 20min all the way to la Balme

From Les Pements, follow a path which runs above but parallel to the road from Hauteluce to Les Saisies and then takes to the road for the last 2km to the resort. Les Saisies was used for the cross-country events in the 1992 winter Olympic Games and the countryside here is of a much more gentle aspect than elsewhere in the region. Go through Les Saisies to the point where the road levels out and follow a track on the right which forks off opposite a car park. Note that there is a war memorial here which carries a plaque in commemoration of a drop of arms to the French resistance by the RAF. The track climbs onto a broad, gently sloping ridge which is followed to the Col de Véry where a small refuge is situated just to the south of the col. During the whole of this day, the western end of the Mt Blanc range is visible ahead of you and gets steadily closer as you walk.

From the col, the route, now a path, descends on the right-hand slopes of the ridge and traverses under the Aiguille Croche. A short, sharp climb up a rocky ridge and another traverse lead to a ridge near the Chalet du Joly from which one quickly descends to the Col Joly itself. There is a restaurant on the col (which can be reached by

---

The Cascade du Reculaz seen from the Sentier à John

road so you will encounter cars here) and another small refuge, Chalet Roselette, a little below the col.

The path continues along the ridge from the Col Joly over grassy slopes with strange craters which suggest that there is gypsum hereabouts, up the steep end of a little ridge, and then makes for the rocks of the Aiguille de Roselette. When you reach a rock barrier, go right, follow a traverse over scree and climb into a little bowl before ascending quickly to the Col de la Fenêtre, which is a square gap in the rocks of the ridge. The slopes above this traverse are full of the *Pulsatilla alpina* anemones, both yellow and white forms, in July. The path descends steeply from the Fenêtre to a junction where you go right, and a second very shortly after where you go left, almost straight down, to the Refuge de la Balme.

Note that if you have split this day and wish to continue to the Col de la Croix du Bonhomme, you should go right at the second junction and avoid the descent to la Balme. Note also that the "official" tour goes round the other side of the Aiguille de Roselette. This reduces the amount of ascent but misses out the Col de la Fenêtre, which would seem to me to be a great pity.

Sixth day: Refuge de la Balme to Refuge du Plan de la Lai

Time needed: 5h

Follow the path up the valley to the Col du Bonhomme, then the Refuge du Col de la Croix du Bonhomme which has recently been improved. This section of path doubles as the Tour du Mt Blanc, Tour du Beaufortain, and G.R.5. It is thus busy.

Turn right at the refuge and head for the impressively sharp ridge of the Crête des Gittes (see Walk No.6 for further details) and follow this to the Col de la Sauce, the chalet at Bel Air and so down to the Refuge du Plan de la Lai.

Seventh day: Plan de la Lai to Refuge de Presset

Time needed: 4h via Col de Bresson or 3h 40min by the Col du Grand Fond. If the latter route is to be used, and if you have stayed at the Refuge du Col de la Croix du Bonhomme, the Presset can be reached in 4h 35min

First alternative via Col de Bresson: Just across the road from the refuge a track goes into the hills. This soon becomes a path which meanders up and down, taking a line roughly parallel with the shore of the Lac de Roselend, which unfortunately is not visible because of the convex slope below you. Eventually, the path descends into the little valley of Treicol and then climbs up the head of this on either path or track. From Presset climb the hillside on the left on a path which goes fairly directly up to the Col de Bresson. Cross the col and take a path on the left which traverses to the Refuge de Presset above its little tarn. This is a pleasant enough route but is unusual for this part of the world in having substantial muddy sections. Nor is it as scenic as the alternative below.

Second alternative via the Col du Grand Fond: Turn left on leaving the refuge and follow the road to the Cormet de Roselend. It is possible to avoid some of the road by using an obvious path which climbs on the right. At the summit of the cormet, a track goes off on the right and traverses around the end of the ridge into a long, straight valley called the Combe de la Neuva. Follow the bottom of the valley until the paths (there are three at different levels - see Walk No.9) take you up the right-hand wall and below the Pointe Presset to the Col du Grand Fond. The view of the Refuge de Presset below, with the odd shape of the rock column of the Pierra Menta behind, is an unforgettable sight. The descent to the refuge is quickly accomplished and presents no difficulty.

If you have stayed the night at the Refuge du Col de la Croix du Bonhomme it is best to descend from the Crête des Gittes to the Cormet de Roselend and follow this second alternative. There are no real paths down the south slopes of the Gittes but the ground is not difficult and several ways can be found.

Eighth day: Refuge de Presset to Bourg St Maurice

Time needed: 6h 10min

From the refuge, descend to the path which leads from the Col de Bresson to the Refuge de la Balme. Note that this is an alternative stopping place to the Refuge de Presset for the previous day, but to reach it needs an extra hour. You have now completed the loop and need only return to the valley. Follow the track down to the bridge above Foran, keep left and take the path to Crête Merry. From here you can descend to Landry via Valezan and Bellentre as at the start of the tour. It is, however, probably better to make straight for Bourg St Maurice. For a while before Crête Merry you may have noticed that the path is following a ditch. This is the old water duct called the Canal des Chapelles and can be followed across the hillside. It crosses two tracks and the second can be used to get easily to Les Chapelles. From there take the road through Montgirod and Vulmix to Bourg. Off-road paths are described in the section on short walks, which do not save any time but may be preferable.

Summary of refuges and Gîtes d'Étape
These are given in the order in which they are encountered during the tour.

La Balme - Altitude 1984m. Meals provided. 25 beds (79 09 70 62 - the Mairi at Aime - for information). Commune d'Aime.

Presset - Altitude 2514m. No guardian. 22 beds. Club Alpin Français.

De la Coire - See Walk No.4.

La Grangette - 1140m. 32 beds (79 38 14 51). Private. Situated above Arêches.

Les Clarines - Altitude 1450m. Breakfast provided. 16 beds (79 38 13 70). Private. Situated at L'Ami St Guérin.

Gîte de Molliesoulaz - Altitude 900m. 18 beds (79 38 02 58). Commune de Queige. Situated on the hillside south of Queige.

Gîte de Pemonts - Altitude 1365m. Meals provided. 16 beds (79 38 83 45). Commune de Hauteluce.

De Bellasta - Altitude 1915m. Meals provided. 16 beds (79 38 10 09). Private. Near Col de Véry.

Chalet Roselette - Altitude 1871m. Meals provided. 15 beds (50 47 13 31). Private. Situated below the Col Joly.

De la Balme - Altitude 1706m. Meals provided. 70 beds (50 47 03 54). Private.

Du Col de la Croix du Bonhomme - Altitude 2443m. Meals provided. 100 beds (79 07 05 28). Club Alpin Français.

Plan de la Lai - See Walk No.6.

De la Nova - See Walk No.6.

Du Lachat - Altitude 1600m. Meals provided. 34 beds (79 31 71 51). Club Alpin Français. Situated north of the Col des Saisies.

8: Col de la Charbonnière (2494m) and Mt Rosset (2449m)

Grade: 3

Map: 3532OT

Time needed: From Foran, for the circuit 5h 30min

Comment: An excellent walk up a valley surrounded by precipices, into alps dominated by the magnificent Pierra Menta, over into the rocky cirque around the Lac de la Portetta and then back via the grassy slopes of Mt Rosset

Approach: By car from Bourg St Maurice, follow the road to Vulmix and continue through the villages of Montgirod, Picolard, Valezan and Montméry. This is in itself a very attractive run with good views of the Bellecôte to the south. It is known as the Balcon de la Tarentaise. Just after Montméry the road takes a sharp bend left, over a bridge, and another road goes off on the right through the village of La Bergerie. Follow this and cross the Ormente stream at the Pont de la Gitte. Continue on the still surfaced road to the open valley ahead. The surface soon deteriorates but good parking is to be found near Foran.

Ascent: Continue along the track which takes you steadily up the valley with the rocky sides of the Rognais on the right and the slabs below the Pointe de Gargan ahead. The track swings left under these slabs and climbs quickly to the Refuge de la Balme (refreshments) and more level ground. Beyond the refuge you are on paths, and there is a fork a little way along where you go right towards the Col de Bresson. Climb a little and then at a convenient point (there is no real path) strike left below the Pierra Menta and aim straight for the col visible at the head of this valley. Some scree needs to be traversed and névé is likely below the col. Eventually, a trace of path will be found which leads through rocky terrain to the summit of the col. Descend towards the lake over rough ground and

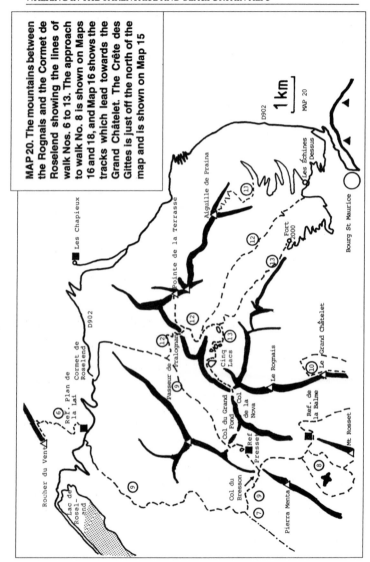

MAP 20. The mountains between the Rognais and the Cormet de Roselend showing the lines of walk Nos. 6 to 13. The approach to walk No. 8 is shown on Maps 16 and 18, and Map 16 shows the tracks which lead towards the Grand Châtelet. The Crête des Gittes is just off the north of the map and is shown on Map 15

then swing round to the east and follow a path which leads towards the slopes of Mt Rosset and the path to the Col du Mt Rosset, which follow north. There is an unmarked path higher up the slopes below the Pointe de Cerdosse which can also be followed and has the advantage that it brings you out near the top of the Col du Mt Rosset. Climb towards the latter and a path will be seen to traverse back to the right across the slopes of Mt Rosset. Follow this to the ridge of the mountain, then follow left to the summit.

Descent: Return to the Col du Mt Rosset from where there are two alternatives. Either cross the col and descent to la Balme and so back to the car, or follow the path south to a track at the Chalet du Mt Rosset which leads, with a deviation on a path through the Bois Borgne, down to the track to Foran. If using this route, note that it is not imperative to return to the Col du Mt Rosset from the summit but that the ridge can be followed south to the chalet without difficulty.

9: Col du Grand Fond (2671m)

Grade:	3 for the last part of the ascent to col, otherwise 2
Map:	3532OT
Time needed:	From Cormet de Roselend to col via Combe de la Neuva 2h 40min. For return via Col de Bresson and Plan de la Lai add 3h 40min
Height gain:	To col 700m, 300m on return
Comment:	A splendid walk along a narrow valley surrounded by rock walls with a dramatic view of the Pierra Menta from the col. The return is over pastoral alps with a view of the Lac de Roselend. This walk is also part of the Tour du Beaufortain

Approach: The walk starts and ends on the top of the Cormet de Roselend, which can be reached by car from either Beaufort or Bourg St Maurice. Alternative starting points are any of the four refuges in the region - Plan de la Lai, la Nova at Les Chapieux, Presset or la Balme.

Ascent: A track leaves the road near one of the car parks and goes south and then east, traversing around the end of a ridge. This takes you into the valley of the Combe de la Neuva, to a structure used for collecting water. Now, either follow the line of the stream or climb up a little to the left, up a broad gully and follow a ledge, almost a subsidiary valley, which runs parallel with the stream and, because of its higher elevation, gives better views. These two ways converge further up the valley and the path then keeps to the right-hand valley wall, or rather paths, since there are three which run parallel, one above the other. You pass near two little tarns (if not still snowbound) and the path swings right, climbing to steep scree slopes below the col du Grand Fond which lead you to its summit with no real difficulty, although there may be substantial amounts of névé. The horizontal crest of the Brêche de Parozan is high on the right and some walkers may be seen on its slopes. Across the valley is the Aiguille de la Nova and Pointe de la Combe Neuve with the Col de la Nova between. This last can be reached from the two tarns by scrambling up a steep scree-filled gully, and while I have not yet done this, we will encounter this place again using a different route in Walk No.13. From the col itself, the principal view is that of the column of the Pierra Menta rising behind the Presset lake and refuge.

From here you can, of course, return by the same route but it is much more satisfying to continue and return to the cormet by the path which runs to the north. To do this, descend the steep path which leads to and passes the Lac de Presset, climb a little to the refuge and then follow the path which traverses over slopes on the right to the Col de Bresson. Cross the col and descend the path to the north-west to the chalets, also called Presset, and into the valley below, now heading north-east. There is, in fact, a track here which zig-zags down and which is easier to follow than the red path marked on the maps - or was the last time I was here. Any path at the time seemed to get lost in alder scrub. Whichever way is chosen, traverse and climb above the Lac de Roselend (which from now on will not always be visible) and follow an undulating shelf which eventually descends gently to a track which leads you to the Plan de la Lai. This path is on both the G.R.5 and the Tour du Beaufortain. It makes a very pleasant walk and is distinguished in being perhaps the only one in the region which brings back memories of my native

Lake District - muddy and wet! From Plan de la Lai, walk back to the cormet up the road, cutting across the big hairpin on a useful path.

10: The Grand Châtelet (2529m)

Grade:	4
Map:	3532OT with approach roads on 3532ET
Time needed:	2h 20min from high chalet, 4h 30min from St Antoine, both times being for complete circuit
Comment:	This is a short walk, though it has some difficult sections and little in the way of paths in its upper parts. Excellent viewpoint for the rocky peaks behind the Rognais. The crenellated ridge of the Rognais dominates the town of Bourg St Maurice. It is ascended by a steep scree gully and has never tempted me to climb it. The ridge that runs due south from the peak ends in two small but graceful pyramids whose ascent we will describe. Further south is a round dôme, nameless on the map, but called locally the Dôme de Vaugelaz

Approach: (1) Take the Balcon de Tarentaise road from Bourg through Vulmix as far as Montgirod and here take the right turn to Les Chapelles. At Les Chapelles, you meet a more or less horizontal road which leads from the village to Couverclaz. Turn sharp left and, after only a few metres, turn right up a track marked as a black line on the map. The way marked through the narrow streets of the village is less practical and is in any case closed to tourist traffic, though the narrow ways of the village are worth having a wander around. You now follow the track for some 6km, taking, high up, the right fork towards Vaugelaz and traversing around the face of the dôme. This leads around the corner to a nameless chalet situated above the ravine of the Arbonne. Park here.

(2) A longer walk can be made by going to Vulmix, turning off to La Thuile and continuing from there on a track which goes to the chalets of St Antoine. Park near the edge of woodland where a path climbs up from the track and follow this onto the ridge ahead and

so onto open ground and to the high chalets already mentioned.

Ascent: Go just below the chalet, cross a little wet ground and pick up a path formed by the remains of an old water canal. This makes a steadily rising traverse of the hillside, arriving quite quickly at a broad gully which takes you to the col between the ridge of the Rognais and the Dôme de Vaugelaz. Now go right and either climb a little bump in the ridge direct by a track made by some 4x4s or traverse below the bump on an obvious path to the right. The latter demands less puff but the former has the better flora. Continue towards the first peak on the ridge (2461m), keeping left in general but always climbing. This peak is climbed face-on and involves a little scramble for the last few metres. The way ahead now looks a little problematical despite looking quite innocuous from the valley below. Descend towards the little pinnacle ahead when a shallow grassy gully will be seen below, to the right. Descend this, looking for a traverse left below the ridge and ignoring the first obvious route, which is a dead-end. Scramble across a short, rocky step and traverse up to regain the top of the ridge on easier ground. Follow the ridge to the Grand Châtelet, your hands being occasionally necessary. The close-up view of the ridge of the Rognais makes an impressive foreground to the maze of ridges beyond.

It is possible to return using the route of ascent but a more exciting finish can be made by continuing in the direction of the Rognais, traversing the right-hand flank of the ridge, and keeping as high as possible but below the rocks of the crest. Progress is barred by a ridge which descends to the right but which contains a gap allowing you to look down into a gully. Some help is given on this traverse by a few traces of paths which are probably made by hunters. Now climb up to the left to a little summit and down the other side to regain the main ridge at the top of the gully (hands again!). Now descend the gully with care. It is full of big scree which does not run - indeed, any attempt to run it could prove fatal - and lower down, water-eroded grooves can also help progress. This unlikely spot shelters a myriad yellow Doronicum flowers and we surprised a chamois on one visit. The gully opens out into a small combe with magnificent walls. Descend to the right over the floor of the combe, and just as the ground steepens again take an obvious path which climbs a little over a rock obstacle and then drops to pick up the canal path. This is now followed without difficulty right back to the starting point.

Note that the gully used for the descent is fairly steep and should not be used if snow-filled, unless, of course, you have the necessary experience and equipment.

11: Aiguille de Praina (2607m)

Grade:	4
Map:	3532ET
Time needed:	Depends on altitude at which you start to walk. We will assume 1800m whence the ascent needs 2h 40min, but Les Échines Dessus (1328m - 4h 20min) or Plan André (1616m - 3h 20min - parking available) are also possible
Comment:	The Praina is the isolated, triangular-faced peak almost due north of Bourg St Maurice and is well worth the climb

Approach: From Bourg St Maurice, take the D902 road in the direction of Les Chapieux. This starts at the roundabout near the station. Follow this past the hairpin bend at Le Châtelard to a point at 954m where a minor road leaves on the left. Follow this to Les Échines Dessus. If continuing from here, drive through the hamlet until you appear to be going to hit a small church. The road does a sort of falling wiggle to the left to avoid the church wall, but you could be forgiven for thinking you had reached an impasse. The track climbs to and past Plan André and there is parking higher up, particularly near an intersection.

Ascent: Walk up the track but avoid the long deviation of the last hairpin by cutting across the hillside and climbing direct to the Chalets de Praina. You are now on a much grazed and well manured alp with the left-hand side of the peak delineated by a rocky ridge known as the Dos du Pachonier. Climb across the alp towards this and make for a grassy rib which goes up the steep face ahead. Climb the rib until a narrow but good path is seen making a climbing traverse across the face of the mountain. Take this and follow it to the right-hand edge of the face where it climbs in zig-zag fashion through some rocks and small cliffs. The path continues faintly near the right-hand edge and brings you to a little gap below the summit whence a few steps land you on the summit platform. Note that there is a traversing path marked on the map but I am not convinced that this corresponds with anything useful on the ground.

Descent: By the same route.

Ornithological note: A pair of bearded vultures which were introduced into the mountains of Haute Savoie a few years ago have taken up residence in the valley of Les Chapieux. On one ascent, we saw them perched in a gap near the top of the Dos du Pachonier. They are so big that for a moment we thought that two people were ahead of us, though in an odd spot. They can occasionally be seen in flight in winter, from the valley floor.

12: Pointe de la Terrasse (2881m)

Grade:	4
Maps:	3532OT for Cormet de Roselend start, also 3532ET for section above Les Échines. D&R No.8
Time needed:	3h 20min from Cormet de Roselend, 5h 10min from Les Échines
Height gain:	914m or 1548m respectively
Comment:	La Terrasse, while not particularly high, is isolated by deep valleys on all sides which adds significance to its stature. The name arises from its appearance from certain viewpoints as being a great, flat summit. Closer acquaintance, however, shows the summit to be an almost horizontal ridge, exposed on both sides. The approach via the Passeur de Pralognan is steep and impressive

Approach: Drive either to the Cormet de Roselend or to the Pont des Moulins across the Charbonnet torrent just beyond Les Échines Dessus, depending on the chosen starting point. If two cars are available, leave one at each point and make the Roselend-Échines traverse, which is the walk I will describe.

Ascent: From the parking point at the Cormet de Roselend, a track leaves due south and works its way around the north-east end of the ridge ahead. This leads to a little dam where the stream's water is collected and diverted elsewhere. Cross the stream to an obvious path which leads on into the Combe de la Neuva but, just above the dam, turn sharp left and climb the slopes above, through a wide gully onto a gently sloping ledge. Cross this, bearing right and following a sometimes indefinite path and making for the scree fan below the wall ahead, which connects the Pointe de Pralognan with the Pointe Noire.

Unlikely as it may seem at this point, the route follows a not too difficult breach in this wall. The path now climbs grass slopes between rock buttresses and scree and becomes more definite. Eventually, it reaches the scree which it climbs steeply with some cairns to help keep to the route. This aims for the foot of a scree gully on the left, and as you reach the foot of the wall, a path will be seen which climbs to the right up broken rocks and then zig-zags vertically to the top of the wall to arrive just to the left of a large cairn.

The terrain is now grassy with the summit of la Terrasse visible above and to the left. To the left of the summit there is a large scree cone with a col on its left. A path goes left towards this col and there takes a rising traverse across the scree, following a line visible from below. The scree is fine and mixed with soil but gives adequate footing. The slope, which from below looks a bit of a slag heap, is packed with *Ranunculus glacialis* which, if in flower, provides a remarkable sight. There is also *Thlaspi rotundifolium*, which is called locally the "Tabouret (stool) des Alps", and some *Linaria alpina* to give extra colour. The path traverses under a big gendarme on the ridge and then ascends a steep scree gully between this and the summit rocks to arrive on a little col. Scramble up the rocks on the ridge on the right for a few metres and then climb to the summit, which is now near, up scree on the left of the rocks, and round to the right to the summit cairn. The rocky ridge ahead can be traversed to its end with care and one can look down from there to the Tarentaise Valley.

Descent: From the summit to the foot of the scree cone by the route of ascent. It is inadvisable to try and run the scree as this is quite a thin layer over the underlying rock. From the foot of the scree you can return via the Passeur to the Cormet de Roselend. Alternatively, you can continue without retracing your steps and follow the Charbonnet Valley to Les Échines. Descend the undulating grassy slopes below, making for the slopes below the Pointe Noire. There are steep cliffs between you and the valley below, with a break under the Pointe Noire. Pass some ruins and descend, following a path marked with red waymarks. This eventually leads across the top of an open gully, then scree slopes, making for the end of the valley below you. Herd paths appear and are followed into the trough of the valley, which is descended, keeping the stream on your right. At the first ruined chalet (Chalet de la Combe) a path climbs up to the right and is the alternative way to the Cinq Lacs. Descend past more ruins, then through what appears to be a ruined hamlet, then steeply aiming for a large rock beside the torrent where a new footbridge will be found. Cross and descend to the track. Follow this to the bottom of the hairpin bend but leave on the right on a path which leads down the valley to the Pont des Moulins. Note that the map is misleading for the last descent before the track is reached. Under no circumstances should the stream be crossed before the big rock as you will get involved in a fight with the alder scrub on the other side of the stream.

13: Cinq Lacs (2532m) and Col de la Nova (2811m)

Grade: 2 to the lakes, 3 to Col de la Nova
Maps: 3532ET and 3532OT - the walk is on the join!
Time needed: From Fort de la Platte 1h 55min to lakes, 2h 50min to col. From Les Échines Dessus 4h and 5h respectively
Comment: This has become, deservedly, a very popular walk. We first did it in 1980 when there was a narrow path, now evolved in places to two wide ones in parallel. It is a walk which caters for all abilities and takes you well into the dramatic scenery behind the Rognais

Approach: (1) Drive to Les Échines Dessus as in Walk No.11 and continue on a track into the Charbonnet Valley, cross the bridge and follow the track up the hillside until it levels out. At Grandville, take

The region of the Cinq Lacs from La Terrasse

the track which climbs up to the right and follow this to the Fort de la Platte. The track is narrow and there are some steep bends but it is not exposed. Park near the fort (refreshments) and remember that the early bird gets the best places.

(2) Park in the Charbonnet Valley, near the bridge.

Ascent (1): From the fort, follow the ridge ahead and paths over easy ground until you drop into a small valley below the Col de Forclaz. Cross the stream and climb to a vantage point overlooking the first of the five lakes. From here you can go up the ridge on the left on a path with a slightly awkward step in it, or descend a little to an obvious path below which meets the first one in a little rocky gully. Lakes 2 and 3 are soon reached and the path skirts them on their right, then turns left between lakes 3 and 4. Much sunbathing and picnicking goes on hereabouts on a good day. The fifth lake, Lac Noir, is reached by a steepish climb up a gully.

During the latter part of this walk it is possible to see ahead a rather imposing, conical peak called la Torche, which is on the left as you make the final climb up to the Lac Noir. In fact, this peak is a bit of a fraud as it is the end of an almost level ridge which can be

143

ascended easily from beside the lake, but which is well worth the slight effort.

The next stage of the walk is to climb to the ridge ahead. This is done either up a path which climbs the slope to the right of the lake or, more interestingly, go to the far end of the lake and follow traces of path up rock ledges where the scree and ordinary ground meet. On the crest of the ridge, where there is plenty of view to admire, turn left and follow the ridge, either along its crest or below the crest on its left, whichever is the easiest. In this way, you climb towards a large, round structure which turns out to be a shelter, and past this to a point just below the steep upper slopes of the Pointe de la Combe Neuve. Here a path goes to the right and makes a few rather airy steps around the top of an exposed gully to land you on the broad shoulder of the col de la Nova. From here one gets a close-up of the Aiguille de la Nova, which is a rock climb. The scree slope on the left descends into a valley which leads to the Foran Valley, while further down the ridge of the col, a scree gully descends on the right into the Combe de la Neuva.

Ascent (2): From Les Échines follow in reverse the route described in Walk No.12 which leads to la Terrasse. Quite high up the Charbonnet Valley, near a chalet, a path will be seen which traverses back across the left-hand side of the valley and climbs to a little gap, soon after which it reaches the first of the lakes and from where the route from the fort is joined.

Descent: By the route used for the ascent. If the car has been left at Les Échines, it is possible to ascend by the Charbonnet and return via the fort. From the fort, leave the track and continue down grassy slopes in the direction of the Fort du Truc and then down to track and car. Note the commanding view these two forts have of the valley, in particular of the crossing into Italy, though I gather that neither was ever involved in any hostilities.

SOME SHORT WALKS

Several fragments of the walks described above make excellent outings for less ambitious days:

1. **The Col de la Fenêtre** from Col Joly is one such outing, with good views of Mt Blanc from both cols and a pleasant flora along the

path. Refreshment is also close at hand on Col Joly. The route is described in Walk No.7, the Tour of the Beaufortain, day 5. Allow up to 1¹/₂h to the col. - *Grade 2.*

2. **The Cormet d'Arêches,** which can be reached by car, can be used as a starting point for three outings. The approach is described in Walk No.3.

3. **Col du Coin,** as described in Walk No.7, day 2, is approached mostly on a track which gives no problems. The path to the col is quite steep. Allow about 1h to the col. - *Grade 2.*

4. **The Croix du Berger,** Walk No.3, is a very attractive walk and requires only about 1h there and back. - *Grade 1.*

5. **The Crête du Boeuf** is a pleasant grassy walk among abundant flora which could easily occupy 2 or 3h of a pleasant day. This is mentioned in Walk No.4. - *Grade 1.*

6. **The Lac des Fées** is a superb and popular picnic spot and is below the cormet on the Arêches side.

    As you wander around here you may notice some large, regularly spaced cavities on the steeper hillsides. These date from the days before electric fences when the cattle were often tethered when grazing. Cattle need to lie down and so it was necessary to cut out a platform for each beast.

7. From Foran, the walk to the **Refuge de la Balme** is not difficult and needs about 1¹/₂h to the refuge. This is described in Walk No.8. - *Grade 1.*

    Many walks are possible on the lower slopes of the valley and some pleasant ones are described below. Map 3532ET.

8. **Les Échines, Tigny and la Pierre à Cupules** - There is a complex of interlinking paths and tracks on the lower slopes of the Aiguille de Praina, the peak immediately north of Bourg St Maurice, and these can be employed to make many walks of different durations. All *Grade 2.*

    Set out on foot from the roundabout near the station at Bourg in the direction of Les Chapieux, pass the pizzeria and take a path which goes directly up the hillside. This momentarily joins a road and then climbs steeply - very steeply for 50m or so - up the hillside, behind a garage. The slope eases as the path enters a groove and takes a climbing traverse right, then left to the hamlet of Les Maisonettes where you reach the road.

First alternative: Turn right and return to Bourg on the road, through Le Villaret and Le Châtelard. There is a short cut on the right above Le Châtelard past a chalet, and a second through the hamlet itself which goes down left among the buildings. Allow 1h 40min for the circuit.

To extend the walk, turn left at Les Maisonettes and take a path on the right a few metres further on. This goes past and behind an isolated chalet and soon reaches the road again.

Second alternative: The path continues across the road, meets and crosses this again, and finally meets it again a little below Les Échines Dessous. Follow the road to the village. Return by the same route. Allow 2^{1}/2h for the circuit.

Third alternative: At the road above the isolated chalet, turn right and follow it to the next hairpin bend. Here, take a track to the right which traverses the hillside to pleasant, secluded pastures at Champ Plan. At the end of the track there is a group of buildings and, though it is not evident from a distance, a path goes between them, makes a sharp left turn and climbs through woods. This fades out on open fields over which a way is made to a track above. Turn left to Les Échines Dessous to arrive near the church. Return by the previous route in 2^{1}/2h.

Fourth alternative: Either continue past the church along the track through the village if you used the second alternative, or turn right on the track if you used the third alternative. The track turns a corner and then descends steadily to the road to Les Chapieux. About half way along, on the right, is a large stone which is indicated by a notice to be la Pierre à Cupules. Prehistoric men have carved dozens of little thimble-shaped holes into the top of the rock, which has probably been chosen for this (religious?) practice because of its commanding position above the valley. When you reach the road, turn right and walk back to Bourg. Allow 3^{1}/2h for the circuit.

For Les Tigny, it is best to drive to Les Échines Dessous and park by the church. Follow the road up to and into Les Échines Dessus, going right through the village. Go past the first hairpin bend and take a track off to the right. This climbs for a while, then traverses right below some rocks onto a more open hillside above the chalets at Les Tigny. Note that a path is marked in red below this route on the TOP25 map which climbs via a steep slope which has recently been cut by a mudslide and, while still practicable, it is not easy to find. From Les Tigny go towards Merindet, then climb through clearings in the woods until it is possible to descend a little and pick up a path which zig-zags down through steep forest to the Les Chapieux road. A little before this is reached a path branches off to the right and takes you to the track back to Les Échines Dessous. (Allow $3^{1/2}$h.)

There is also a very pleasant circuit which crosses the hillside below the Fort du Truc. Start near the pizzeria and climb the path to Les Échines Dessous, then by road to Les Échines Dessus. As you reach the village, take a track to the left which quickly brings you to a bridge over the Charbonnet river. Immediately over this bridge, a track turns off left and follows the river, descending slowly. This is followed until you reach a concrete slab. The track continues but here it is necessary to descend onto the pastures and follow a faintly marked path which brings you to some small quarry-like workings. Below and to the right is a ruined chalet among trees. Aim below this and find a path which takes you across a little stream and onto a much better marked path. The terrain is confusing since the paths are criss-crossed by cattle trods. The path across the stream takes you down to a track which is climbed to the chalets at Le Replatet. Go through the buildings and pick up a path which descends in zig-zags to the hamlet of La Rosière, above Bourg. Follow the road down to the starting point. (Allow 3h for the circuit.)

9. **Vulmix-Parchet-Les Chapelles** - Drive to Vulmix from Bourg St Maurice. At the approach to the village, the road makes a wide, right-hand bend and crosses an old track, the right-hand branch being surfaced. Park near here. Alternatively, you can walk from Bourg, turning uphill at the traffic lights opposite the gendarmerie. The path is signposted and takes you into Vulmix. Turn left to reach the crossroads.

Follow the track, which is almost horizontal, away from Vulmix across the hillside to the hamlets of Parchet and Feindaille and then join the D87 road. There is a short cut path on the right just after Feindaille. Climb this road to a junction with the balcony road linking Picolard with Montgirod. Here there are two possibilities, the shortest route being to go right to Montgirod along the road. Go just past the turning to Les Chapelles and take a rising track on the left which passes a chalet with a "Gîtes de France" sign. Follow this track, keeping right at a 'Y' junction, and descend gently to Vulmix through a wooded gully. The second, and longer possible route is to go left for a few metres on the balcony road and then climb a steep mule track on the right. This leads directly to the village of Les Chapelles, crossing the road just below the village. Go straight up to the top of the village and turn right along a track. Cross a little stream and take a path on the right which descends into the woods near the gully, where you turn sharp right on a track which meets the track from Montgirod at the 'Y' junction. - *Grade 1* via Montgirod; *Grade 2* via Les Chapelles.

CHAPTER 5:
Les Chapieux to the Nant Cruet

INTRODUCTION

As will be seen from the map of this part of the Tarentaise, there is a continuous mountain ridge which runs from the Col de la Seigne north-east of Les Chapieux, via the Col du Petit St Bernard to and beyond the Nant Cruet Valley and which always exceeds 2567m in altitude except at the Col du Petit St Bernard. The ridge forms the frontier with Italy. The northerly part runs south at first with several rocky peaks exceeding 3000m, then turns more to the east, with peaks between 2800 and 3000m in altitude, rounded at first in general appearance but becoming impressively jagged as you near the Glacier of the Rutor; les Dents Rouges with the satellite Œillasse, the Pointe du Tachuy, the Grand Assaly with its sharp finger sticking out of the western ridge and the Pointe du Grande. The ridge now swings into a southerly direction again and the peaks all become higher, exceeding 3000m and culminating in the Aiguille de la Grande Sassière, which at 3747m is the third highest in the Tarentaise.

A complex of ridges runs from this backbone and reaches into French territory to produce a number of magnificent cirques with walking either within each or interconnecting over the spur ridges or with Italy over the cols. Starting in the north, there is the Fornet and Beaupré, then south of the Col du Petit St Bernard is the Combe des Moulins, which is part of the ski area of La Rosière, though the uplift is relatively inconspicuous here. Next is the smaller valley of the Jourdan and then the bowl of La Sassière from which the skyline is very attractive, with rocky peaks and the glacier of the Invernet spilling over from the edge of the Rutor glacier. The ridge of Montséti separates the Sassière from the less dramatic scenery of the Vallon de Mercuel and the walker can pass from one valley to the other over this ridge via the Lac Noir. These last three valleys are served by a road from Ste Foy which passes through La Masure and the very pretty hamlet of Le Crot. Note that there is a climbing outcrop below Le Crot with parking at Plan du Pré.

The next valley south is again large and is enclosed by its ridges to form almost a sanctuary. It is reached via Ste Foy la Thuile and the protected hamlet of Le Monal with its meadows, tarns and

MAP 21. The region described in Chapter 5 showing the main access roads and the layout of the ridges separating France and Italy

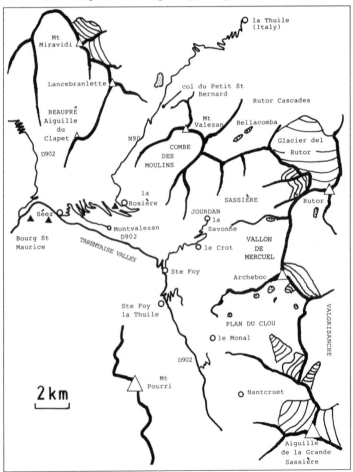

surrounding short walks. The chalets of the hamlet are spread out and have recently had their enamelled steel roofs replaced by the more traditional lauzes or thin rock slabs. There is a small chapel sprouting from its rock of ages and a refuge. This is an ideal place for a family outing and picnic. The foot of the valley above hangs over Le Monal and its presence is not evident from below because of the steep approach slopes. Once these are surmounted, though, the walker finds him or herself looking into a broad, flat plain, the Plan du Clou. The slopes of the ridge to the left lead to lakes and summits while straight ahead are two high cols from which there are views into Italy. Round the corner, to the right, it is possible to walk up to the moraine plains of the glaciers of les Balmes. These glaciers are quite spectacular with two upper tongues hanging over the valley. From time to time, these discharge a great load of ice which is pulverised as it falls and then reconsolidates to form the lower glacier, a feature which is not easy to see as it is covered with rock debris. Needless to say, you should not approach too closely below the upper glaciers. The whole valley is full of flowers in season.

There was at one time a project to build a dam and flood the Plan du Clou but this, happily, has been abandoned. The service roads remain as scars on the hillsides but these have now mostly been reseeded and are already becoming less evident.

The last valley on this side of the ridge is the curiously Welsh sounding Nant Cruet. This is reached either from Le Monal or via Les Pigettes and the hamlet of Chenal. It is a straight V-shaped valley with an opening at its head into a bowl below the Glacier de la Sassière which descends from the Aiguille of the same name.

On the Italian side of the main ridge is the Valgrisanche (also spelled Valgrisenche) which from its head under the Aiguille de la Grande Sassière runs more or less north. The western slopes of the valley are steep and precipitous except where a side valley runs up to the Col du Mont and the Lago di San Grato below the Testa del Rutor.

Several maps are required to cover this region completely. In the 1:50,000 series both D&R Nos.8 and 11 are needed, the former being the only one of the new series of maps which shows the region around the Lagi di Bellacomba in the north. In the 1:25,000 TOP25 series, the part of the region north of Mt Valezan is covered by No.3531ET and the southern part by No.3532ET. The Bellacomba are on the old and superseded IGN map Série Bleue No.3632 ouest, if you happen to have one, though this is not now available. The small part of the Valgrisanche not on the TOP25 map is covered by the Italian IGC series No.102.

The walks will be described starting from the north.

1: Col de Faux Ouillon (2780m)

Grade:	2
Map:	3531ET
Time needed:	2h 50min. Add 1h if starting from L'Orgière
Height gain:	830m
Comment:	This is a col which is not used as a crossing place but which is a magnificent belvedere for close views of the Mt Blanc range. It is also situated under the summit of les Grandes Aiguilles

Approach: Drive north from Bourg St Maurice towards Les Chapieux on the D902. The road makes a series of 10 hairpin bends, levels out and turns a right-hand corner to pass near the hamlet of Crêt Bettex. A track goes off right and climbs to the hamlet of L'Orgière which is one possible starting point. The track, however, continues in good enough state as far as La Vacherie and you can start here, or indeed at any intermediate point.

Ascent: Just before La Vacherie, the track crosses a stream which runs down a little gully and which we will climb. To reach it, go past the buildings and climb onto the hillside on the left and traverse back into the foot of the gully. This is steep but short and takes you onto level ground with a path which follows approximately the edge of the steep slope on the right. Ahead, there is a rock bar with a stream flowing through an obvious gap. Make for this and follow a path which climbs to the left, then right of the stream and emerges in the gently sloping upper part of the valley of the Vacherie stream. Follow this without difficulty towards the col, only the last 200m ascent being at any angle.

Descent: By the same route.

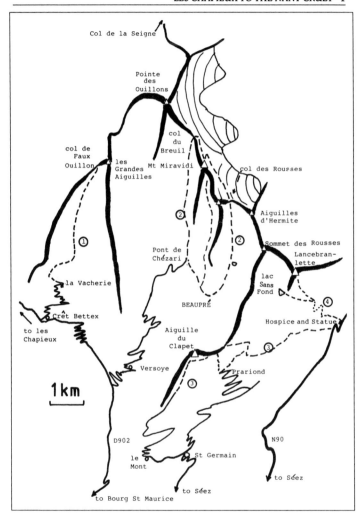

MAP 22. The mountains north of the Col du Petit St Bernard showing the lines of walk Nos. 1 to 4

2: Mt Miravidi (3066m) and the three cols: du Breuil, des Veis and des Rousses

Grade:	4
Map:	3531ET
Time needed:	4h 10min to summit, 6h 50min for circuit
Height gain:	1240m then 50m
Comment:	Mt Miravidi is situated on the Franco-Italian border roughly north-west of the Col du Petit St Bernard. Both it and the Col du Breuil are visible from Bourg St Maurice, behind and to the left of the Aiguille du Clapet. The mountain has two names, Miravidi, the preferred one, being of Italian extraction, and the alternative, Mirande, being French. The mountain has a number of attractive satellites, Aiguille des Veis, Aiguille de Beaupré, Aiguilles de l'Hermite and the Sommet des Rousses. The peaks on the frontier ridge all exceed 3000m and there is a glacier on the Italian side. There is little permanent snow on the French side but névé is likely to be encountered. There are three cols in the ridge and all provide access to the Miravidi from the French side. We will provide descriptions of ascents via the Cols du Breuil or des Veis with the return via the Col des Rousses. The latter involves crossing the glacier névé on the Italian side so that good, substantial footwear is essential. This is normally no problem, though if the ice is bare of névé, the crossing should not be attempted

Approach: From Bourg St Maurice drive towards Les Chapieux as far as Bonneval les Bains, which is in fact an incompleted hotel, neglected for many years. Take the road on the right which is signposted to Versoye (spelling variable) and climbs the steep hillside into the valley above. This is one of the most difficult roads in the area. It is narrow and traverses steep grass slopes without the benefit of any protection. It is the key to an excellent walk but should be used with respect. A little after you have passed Versoye, the road becomes a track, though one that is less exposed. Drive past a ruined barracks to a bend at 1821m where there is parking and a path visible a little below. It is possible to drive as far as the Pont de Chézari at 2047m but this involves another 5km of rough track and the time gained is very little. The Cascade de Beaupré is a fine sight across the valley from here. Note also the position of the cliffs on its left.

Ascent: via the Col des Veis, drop down from the bend to the path below and follow this up the valley above an impressive gorge. This eventually leads you to the level, upper part of the valley near the Pont de Chézari. Cross the bridge and go right towards the chalets at Les Crottes. The entrance to the valley of Méchandeur, which you need to climb, is narrow and is guarded by a line of low cliffs up on the left. Swing left around the grassy bowl ahead to pick up a path which traverses above the cliffs and across a steep grassy slope. This quickly turns into a small valley below the rocks of the Aiguille de Beaupré and the path scrambles through scree, eventually taking to a little ridge on the left to avoid some big blocks in the valley bottom. The ridge is followed to a little summit and then you tend left under and around a series of rocky bosses, keeping more or less parallel with the frontier ridge above until easier ground leads you onto the Col des Veis. Mt Miravidi is then only a short climb up a path through scree on your left. The summit is roomy with a steep drop off the western side, and excellent views of the eastern Tarentaise, Mt Blanc, the Matterhorn, etc.

Via the Col du Breuil, turn left at the Pont de Chézari and quickly take to the slopes on the right, making for the valley below the big cliffs which define the ridge that runs south from Mt Miravidi. The path comes and goes but keep parallel with the cliffs until you arrive at the Col du Breuil. From here follow either the ridge on the right or the glacier to the summit. This col is a very obvious 'U' between the summits whereas the Col des Veis, being higher, is more a depression on the frontier ridge.

Descent: This is possible from any of the three cols, but it is much more pleasant to make a circuit by returning via the Col des Rousses. This is visible from Mt Miravidi to the south-east as a narrow gap between the Aiguille des Veis and the Aiguilles de l'Hermite. Descend to the Col des Veis and take to the glacier, making a descending traverse left so as to avoid steep rock and snow which lies below the frontier ridge. (You should be much lower than the route taken by skiers shown on the TOP25 map.) Aim for the 2800m contour and then climb the 50 or so metres to the col on easy snow slopes. The valley on the other side of the col curves to the right and its bottom, being somewhat sheltered from the sun, has a significant névé cover. Start to descend to the right to avoid big scree and then follow the trough of the valley, using the névé to assist the descent. As you descend you will see below on the left the flat plain which is called the Beaupré. Do not go down to this but keep up on the right on hummocky ground and follow a complex of herd paths round the end of the ridge of les Petites Rousses. Les Crottes soon comes into view and hence the path back to the car.

During the lower part of the descent of the valley, a feature will be observed which traverses the opposite wall and makes its way below the steep rocks of the Aiguille du Clapet and which could well be a path. This is the Ancien Canal du Pain Perdue, now abandoned. The part below the Clapet is overgrown with alder scrub and is no longer practicable as a path.

3: Aiguille de Clapet (2615m)

Grade: 2 to ridge, 4 over rocks to summit
Map: 3531ET though the approach roads are on 3532ET
Time needed: 1h 30min to 2h 30min depending on starting point
Comment: The Aiguille de Clapet is the very sharp pointed peak visible from around Bourg St Maurice, to the left of the gap of the Col du Petit St Bernard. It is a curious mountain since the top consists of two parallel ridges, one grassy and one rocky and crowned by the rocky summit. In between these two ridges is enclosed a small valley with no outlet and in which are found either névé or little lakes, depending on season. The climb to this valley is not difficult though the slopes are steep. On the other hand, the section up the final rocks of the peak is definitely a scramble where hands are

needed to reach the airy summit. Though short, the ascent is well worthwhile

Approach: The Clapet is climbed either from near the top of the Col du Petit St Bernard or from starting points on the slopes above Séez. For the first, park near the statue of St Bernard, which is situated above a double hairpin bend. A path, now enlarged to a track, is signposted at the bottom of these bends and makes a gently rising traverse, then turns up a stream for a little way before making its way across steep grassy slopes towards the Col de Forclaz. Note that higher up this route has been confused somewhat by the construction of a new track, which you do not wish to use.

For the second approach, take the road which leads from Séez to the Col du Petit St Bernard as far as Villard Dessus where a road goes off to the left just after a restaurant. This climbs through the village and steeply up through pastures (ignore a right turn just before a tree-lined alley), over a bridge and up a series of hairpins to the hamlet of St Germain. The road divides here. To the left it goes to the hamlet of Le Mont and thence to a picnic area at an altitude of 1522m. From here a track climbs to Montagne du Plan and then Combottier. The south-west ridge of the Clapet is climbed from here. Alternatively, take the right fork at St Germain and follow the road, then track in the direction of the Petit St Bernard. Hereabouts you are on, or near, the old Roman road over the col which was used until about 1860, when the modern road was built. The track continues all the way to the col but at an altitude of 1867m there is a track which leaves sharply on the left. (The map is deceptive here as this is a junction of tracks, not track and path.) A track rises in a series of hairpins to the semi-ruined buildings at Prariond. The ascent can be started anywhere between St Germain and Prariond.

Ascent: From Prariond, an initially poor track climbs to the right. Follow this a little way and then traverse left and right onto a path system. You will now see ahead, in the direction of the St Bernard, a small rounded bump with a little rock pinnacle on its right. Make for the rear of the bump and follow a path which traverses the hillside and eventually joins the path from the St Bernard road already described. Go left to the Col du Forclaz. It is equally possible to go straight up from the bump. There are no paths but the climb follows folds in the ground and the side of a little gully and arrives on the ridge above the hidden summit valley.

From Combottier, follow paths on the steep grass ridges ahead and when beneath the summit rocks of the Clapet, traverse to the right over big scree blocks to enter the hidden valley.

It is, in fact, possible to climb the Clapet up the broken rocks and scree visible from this point, and you may well see parties using this way. It is, however, almost impossible to describe and there is a much better way. Cross the valley to the foot of the opposite wall and with the rocks of the Clapet on your left. A slope of scree and blocks will be seen rising to a small gap. Climb to the gap and wend a way through and over large blocks onto a little terrace. Keep to the right (near the abyss) and cross the terrace towards a shallow gully which leads to the shoulder above and to a level space with more blocks. Climb towards and to the left of the summit until it is possible to scramble up the last few blocks to the sharp peak, which has room for perhaps four walkers. The ascent from the hidden valley is both spectacular and exposed and for the confirmed walker is approaching the domain of the rock climber. The climb is, nevertheless, within the capabilities of any fit and experienced party.

Descent: Use the line of ascent over the rocks and from the hidden valley either the route of ascent or follow partly one of the alternatives, as is convenient.

4: The Lancebranlette (2936m) & Lac Sans Fond (2456)

Grade:	2 with one short passage of 3
Map:	TOP25 3531ET
Time needed:	2h 40min
Height gain:	784m
Comment:	The Lancebranlette is situated on the Franco-Italian frontier and is the first peak to the west of the Col du Petit St Bernard. It has the distinction of being recommended in the Michelin green guide for the Alps and so attracts more than its fair share of walkers. The starting point is, of course, easily accessible from the N90 road to the col

View to the Italian frontier from the Lancebranlette

Approach: Drive towards the col and park near the Ancienne Hospice at an altitude of 2153m.

Ascent: A path leaves the road making straight for the peak, crosses a stream and then zig-zags up the hillside ahead. It eventually crosses a slope of shaly scree which requires some care (*Grade 3*) and then climbs onto the ridge of the mountain, which is ascended without difficulty on a good path worn to a deep groove in the turf. This is an excellent viewpoint with a "table d'orientation" just below the summit.

Descent: By the same route. The walk may be prolonged by taking a path to the right (as you descend) below the passage over the scree. This traverses grass slopes to the Lac Sans Fond nestling in its combe dominated by the sharp point of the Roc de Belleface. The slopes by the path contain one of the biggest concentrations of spring gentians I have ever seen and there are swathes of *Aster alpinus* on the slopes above. A favourite picnic spot. Return by the same path to the hospice.

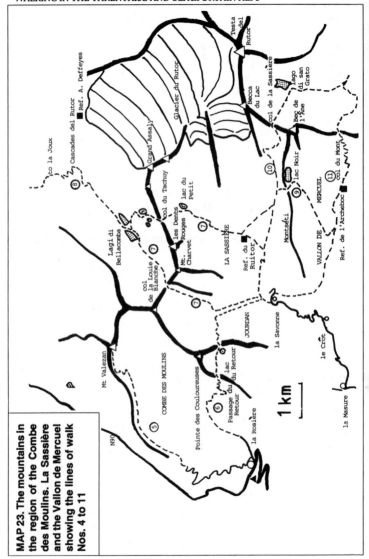

MAP 23. The mountains in
the region of the Combe
des Moulins, La Sassière
and the Vallon de Mercuel
showing the lines of walk
Nos. 4 to 11

5: Mont Valezan (2891m)

Grade: 2 with a short section at 4
Map: 3531ET
Time needed: 2h 30min, easily extended
Height gain: 730m
Comment: A short and pleasant walk with excellent views

Approach: Drive up to La Rosière on the N90 but just before the resort take a sharp turn right to Les Eucherts. After 400m a track goes off to the left and meanders its way to the Roc Noir. It is rough but adequate for a car and there is good parking near the top of a ski tow below the Roc. It is equally possible to start the walk from Les Eucherts (add 1h to the time) or, on certain days, to take the chair-lift from La Rosière.

Ascent: Follow the track parallel with the ridge which hides the road to the Col du Petit St Bernard (viewpoint on the ridge on the left) as far as the Col de Traversette. Here there is a ruined fort, la Redoute Ruinée, whose history is given on a board by the entrance. In 1940, the Italians had joined the war against the French and were attacking their alpine defences. The Redoute Ruinée was under the command of Captain Desserteaux, whose name has been given to a street in Bourg St Maurice. They resisted strongly and successfully. An armistice was signed to come into effect on the 25th of June but it was not until the 3rd of July that the garrison received the order to leave - which they did, bearing their arms with a guard of honour formed by Italian mountain troups.

From the col a well made path can be seen which traverses horizontally east until a path leaves on the left and climbs up into a shallow combe. Follow this to the ridge and continue towards Mt Valezan. Eventually the ridge steepens near the peak and it becomes necessary to scramble up a short gully before arriving at the top. Make careful note of the route since there is a false gully on your right which must not be taken on the descent.

Descent: By the same route. However, from the Col de Traversette, the map suggests a number of different return routes which can be used to prolong the walk into the Combe des Moulins. The precise alternative to choose if this is done will depend to some extent upon where the car has been left.

6: Lac du Retour (2397m) via Passage du Retour

Grade:	3 due to steepness of path
Map:	3532ET
Time needed:	2h 10min
Height gain:	537m
Comment:	A steep path leading to a lake nestling in an attractive hollow.

Approach: Drive to Les Eucherts as in Walk No.5.

Ascent: Follow the track to Putretruit and descend a path into the Moulins Valley, cross the stream and climb through alder scrub to the buildings at Plan Pigeux. The route now follows the broad, steep gully above the buildings which is reached by a rising traverse right and then left to join the zig-zags in the gully. From the top it is only a short walk to the lake.

Alternative ascent: This starts at the village of Le Châtelard (1400m) which is easily reached from the N90 road to La Rosière by turning off at the junction marked with altitude 1593m on the TOP25 map. The village is easy to recognise because of its white church placed on a rocky knoll. This is the Chapel St Michel, built in a most impressive setting, and much photographed with the glaciers of the Mt Pourri group behind. A horizontal track from the village traverses to Roset in the bottom of the Combe des Moulins from where there are good paths direct to Plan Pigeux. This variation increases the height gain to 997m and time to 3h 20min.

Descent: By either route. A longer alternative is also possible. Just east of the lake there is a col, the Col du Retour (2419m), from which you look into the unnamed valley which the locals name after some ruins at its entrance - the Jourdan. A good path, which is not marked on the maps, descends more or less directly into this valley and follows the stream to La Savonne. A mixture of path and road then takes you to Le Crot, from where you can return to Le Châtelard via Le Miroir and Les Moulins using a steep path through fields (dashed line on map) which takes you up to the village. I am reluctant to recommend the whole circuit since not only does it add a further 3 miles (4.8km) to the total distance and involves another 200m of ascent at the end of the day, but there is a lot of road walking, possibly in the heat of the day. If, however, your party has two cars, leave one at Le Crot and the other at the starting point, Les Eucherts or Le Châtelard, so that the road section can be missed out.

7: Tour of the Dents Rouges

Grade: 4. The Col de la Louie Blanche can be evasive and part of the ascent to, and all the descent from, the col are trackless

Map: 3532ET covers part or D&R No.8

Time needed: 5h 50min

Height gain: 796m to Col de la Louie Blanche then 299m to the Col du Tachuy, or 1095m in all

Comment: A delightful walk through some of the most attractive scenery in this part of the range. It demands an experienced party capable of finding the way without paths, and névé will be encountered early in the season. Part of the route is in Italy and passports should be carried. You are unlikely to be asked for them but it can happen

Approach: Drive to Ste Foy on the road to Val d'Isère. If driving up the valley, pass through the village centre and follow a long left-hand bend. Just as you emerge from this there is a signposted turning on the left. Follow this to La Masure (just before Le Miroir) and turn right at a road signposted to La Sassière. This is narrow but surfaced and takes you up through Le Crot and up to La Savonne. A new car park is signposted just before La Savonne but many people park a little higher. Note that a little before La Savonne the road swings sharp left by a big rock; do not go straight on.

Ascent: Walk up the road until it crosses the stream just before La Savonne. Turn left (sign La Sassière) and follow a good track until it forks. Take the left fork (the right is again signposted). There are now two possible routes. One is to cross to the west bank of the

163

stream and follow the track mentioned in Walk No.6 to the Col du Retour. There is then said to be a traversing track to the right around the head of the valley which eventually peters out. A French party I met say that this is straightforward enough. I have used the other route in which you keep to the east of the stream and scramble past the remains of a recent rockfall. Once past this a trace of a path zig-zags up on the right, close to a small stream bed, and reaches a path which climbs along the valley side. (This starts at La Vacherie d'en Bas, but is also cut by the rockfall and, I suspect, is now less used.) Follow this towards the head of the valley. It peters out on a small grassy plateau above the stream. Find a way through the rocky slope above to another level area and continue up and to the right using the ground to best advantage. Some trace of path will eventually be discovered which leads to the col. Evidently, map and compass are essential equipment. The top of the col is broad and flat and surrounded by wild country. I saw chamois on the way up; there is certainly plenty of room for them here and little chance of disturbance outside the hunting season.

The route now descends the valley ahead into Italy. The ground is covered with big scree which demands a great deal of boulder hopping. The two Lagi di Bellacomba are not visible at first due to an intervening ridge on the left but come into view as you work your way round this. The going can be quite awkward at times where the blocks are big but patches of névé will be found to ease the way considerably. Above, on the right, are the slopes below the Dents Rouges while ahead the two lakes sparkle in their splendid setting. The upper lake is bounded by steep cliffs on its north-west side and it seems impossible to pass that way. In the centre of the lake is an island with equally precipitous sides and not much in the way of landing points. The scree extends to the other banks of the lake and as you descend, keeping the lake necessarily on your left, a path will appear above the southern shore. Follow this to the foot of the lake and then turn right along a path which almost immediately climbs up the hillside to the south. If in doubt, climb a little bump to the right of the path which will bring the new path into view, and cross it. The path climbs in zig-zags up to two small lakes, avoiding crags as it does so, and follows the shore of the first, keeping the lake on the left (alt. 2549m) then climbs up a slope to the second (2569m) which it keeps on the right. The path is now less definite and continues across stony ground (or névé) in a rising, right-hand traverse making for the lowest part of the ridge, quite close to the Dents Rouges.

Once there you are on the Col du Tachuy. The rocky ridge on the left rises in a series of summits towards the Glacier of the Rutor and the Testa del Rutor is visible to the rear, while the rock spires of the Œllasses are ahead.

The climbing is now over and only descent remains. Go straight down from the col on steep ground on path or névé making for the right of the Lac du Petit. The path scrambles among boulders along the shore and leads to a flat area very popular for high altitude picnics. A good but very rough path leads down from the lake, keeping well above the stream at first and then dropping toward a little green oasis at the confluence of two streams. (This point can equally be reached by passing the Petit Lac du Petit, going to the Plan du Grand and descending by the Nant Grillotan where there is also a path.) The bed of the stream has been blocked here by large boulders through which it threads its way. These blocks are used to

The Grand Assaly from the Col du Tachuy

cross the stream. Note that there is a false path which continues for a short way without crossing. Follow the real path by the stream down to a small bridge and the plain of La Sassière where, a little way along, you will find the Refuge du Ruitor, the name spelt, naturally, in the French way. Here it is possible to obtain refreshments. Continue along the track across the plain, to where it rises a little by a small chapel, then follow the long descent towards La Savonne. It is possible to avoid the lower part of the track on a path which goes off to the right approximately abreast of La Vacherie d'en Bas which is visible across the valley to the right. This shortly joins the route up the Jourdan Valley which you took in the morning.

We should note in passing that La Savonne is an ideal place for a picnic with distant views towards the Mt Pourri group, and that there is a small restaurant at Le Crot.

8: Les Cascades du Rutor

Comment: The river which emerges from the Glacier du Rutor flows through some impressive rocky terrain to reach a valley which runs at right angles to its direction of flow. Here it leaps down the valleyside and reaches the bottom in two great bounds totalling over 220m in height. Further, lesser waterfalls occur below the main one and above the hamlet of La Joux at the end of the road from La Thuile. The waterfalls are a magnificent sight and are well worth a visit, which can be made either as a variation of the walk just described or as a simple day outing from La Joux.

Note that passports are now essential

8a: Variant of Walk No.7

Grade: 4
Time needed: Les Eucherts - La Joux, 4h 45min
Height gain: 740m

Ascent: Leave the car at Les Eucherts (approached as for Walk No.5) and climb the Passage du Retour to the col of the same name (Walk No.6). Traverse round to the Col de la Louie Blanche and descend to the Lagi di Bellacomba. The track passes between the two lakes (there is a notice here which informs those coming up from the direction of the waterfalls that this is the end of the path) and descends steadily. Ignore a path which descends steeply and keep left on a good path which takes you to a bridge over the river where the noise of the waterfall will already be audible. Take the path over the edge and descend steep zig-zags beside the waterfall. There are one or two points where side paths permit you to approach closely to the cascade. Eventually, the path levels out and takes you along the river, past the other waterfalls and to a restaurant at the end of the road near La Joux. It is then 4km by road to La Thuile where a taxi can be taken back to Les Eucherts. A two-car party can, of course, leave a car at each end of the walk. It is possible to park at the restaurant at La Joux but you are expected, not unnaturally, to patronise the restaurant if this facility is used. The Italian wines are an interesting change from the French.

8b: The Waterfalls alone, or up to the Lagi di Bellacomba

Grade: 2

Time needed: 1h 50min to top of waterfall, 1h from there to Lagi di Bellacomba

Height gain: 540m to top of waterfall, 770m to lake

Approach: Drive over the Col du Petit St Bernard to La Thuile in Italy. Turn right a little before crossing the river in the village and follow the river south through woods until you reach the restaurant at La Joux (see comment above about parking). The path leaves on the left and is easily followed to the foot of the final waterfall at which point it steepens appreciably and zig-zags up the valley side with detours to enable a close look to be taken at the falls. From the top it is possible to prolong the walk as far as the Lagi di Bellacomba on continuing good paths. Alternatively, it is possible to visit the Refuge A. Deffeyes near the foot of the Rutor glacier.

Descent: By the same route.

9: The Montséti Lac Noir (2483m)

Grade:	2
Map:	3532ET
Time needed:	2h 25min for ascent, 1h 30min for descent
Height gain:	712m
Comment:	This is one of several Lacs Noir, and is one of the more popular and so sometimes busy. The Montséti ridge descends from the flank of the Bec de l'Âne and runs in a westerly direction. The lake is situated below the crest of the ridge, and on its south side, and is entirely enclosed by higher ground except at its eastern end where, however, the snow field of the Bec may extend right into the water. The lake has no apparent outlet. It is another good place for a high altitude picnic. The walk described can be done in either direction or it can be combined with either of the two walks Nos.10 and 11

Approach: Start from La Savonne as described for Walk No.7.

Ascent: Follow the path which is signposted to La Sassière and starts just after the point where the road crosses the stream near La Savonne, in the direction of the Jourdan Valley. At the fork, which is again signposted, go right and climb to the track which gives access to La Sassière. This steepens near the top and then levels out near a small chapel. The track then descends to the plain of La Sassière but you need to go right on a short track which leads to a small dam marked as *prise d'eau* on the map. It is normally possible to cross the river here and follow an obvious path which climbs the slope on the other side of the river. Alternatively, continue to La Sassière, cross to the ruined hamlet, and climb a second path up the slope. The two paths join on less steep ground at an altitude of about 2280m. Continue to ascend with the Montséti on the right until a little col becomes evident in the ridge. Climb to this on a scree path among slabs. This is north-facing and often is covered by névé early in the season. The Lac Noir is below on the left.

Descent: The path continues until it reaches the top of an open, rocky gully and the normal route is to descend this until another path is seen traversing off to the right. However, the upper path continues, being very obvious at first but changing quickly into a green path, which appears to be a disused mule track, and which is sometimes difficult to distinguish among the general herbage. The two routes eventually meet up and traverse above the group of hamlets near Le Bochet. The path then turns sharp left and descends a grassy rake which leads to a good track. You are now in the Vallon de Mercuel. Turn right and follow the track until some chalets are reached where a path will be seen going right and tending slightly upwards at first. Follow this across open ground and then into woodland where it descends through very pleasant glades with shade from the afternoon sun. Eventually, open ground is reached again and the path traverses round the end of the Montséti to La Savonne, meeting the La Sassière track a short way above the hamlet.

If the track down the Vallon de Mercuel is followed, this leads steeply to Le Crot. Note also that on the TOP25 map the descent from the Lac Noir is shown as starting from the east of the lake. I have never seen a path here, if indeed it exists.

10: Col de la Sassière (2841m)

Grade:	3
Map:	3532ET
Time needed:	3h 35min
Height gain:	1070m
Comment:	A col situated magnificently under the dark buttresses of the Rutor with a view down to the Lago di San Grato. The col is at high altitude and névé is likely

Approach: Start from La Savonne as for Walk No.7.

Ascent: Take the direction for the Lac Noir as described for Walk No.9 but instead of climbing up to the right to the lake, carry on into a gap between the Becca du Lac and the Bec de l'Âne. As the way steepens, turn left into a funnel-shaped scree slope where a path will be found which leads eventually back into the centre of the upper combe. Tend to the right on névé and make for the frontier ridge to the right of the true col.

Descent: By the same route or via the Lac Noir. This can be reached by traversing over the névé to the crest of the Montséti ridge where it overlooks the lake and following the ridge to its junction with the route of Walk No.5. The ridge is quite exposed and narrow and requires care. From there return by either La Sassière or the Mercuel.

11: Col du Mont (2636m)

Grade:	2 but steep in upper part
Map:	3532ET
Time needed:	2h 55min
Height gain:	865m
Comment:	A pleasant walk with good views into the Gran Paradiso region from the col. The Mercuel Valley will be bright with the yellow anemone in July and the white St Bernard's lily also grows there en masse, beside the track on the way up to La Motte

Approach: Drive to La Savonne as described for Walk No.7.

Ascent: Walk through the hamlet of La Savonne and continue a little way on the track until a path goes off on the right and leads through woods to the Vallon de Mercuel. Go left when this reaches the track coming up from Le Crot and follow this to the hamlet of La Motte, where there is a refuge with refreshments available. A good path climbs up behind and to the right of the hamlet and leads without difficulty to the col, though getting steeper as you near the top.

Descent: By the same route. Alternatively, looking west into France, you can see a broad gully on the right which descends towards La Motte and a path which traverses right about half way down. This allows you to reach the Lac Noir without losing too much height and is recommended in some French texts, though I have not used this route myself. It involves climbing up to the Lac Noir path over easy enough terrain but with little evidence of path.

Extension of Walk over two cols

Grade:	4
Time needed:	Adds at least 3h to the walk
Height gain:	666m

Descend into Italy on a path which is initially indefinite but which becomes good after passing a ruined building not marked on the map. This descends quickly then contours round the hillside to the left and crosses a bridge over a stream. Climb a little and take a path to the left which leads to the Lago di San Grato. From there climb the névé of the Glacier de la Sassière making for a point a little left of the true col. The ascent is steep and should only be undertaken by a party confident and experienced on névé. An ice axe could be useful. The route should not be attempted if the glacier ice is bare. Return by the routes described in Walk No.10.

12: Tour de l'Archeboc

Grade: 3

Maps: 3532ET (IGN) and 102 (IGC)

Time needed: This is a long walk which requires one or two nights in refuges.

Comment: The walk sets out via the Plan du Clou, the next valley south of the Mercuel, and crosses the Col du Rocher Blanc, which from the Italian side is called the Col du Vaudet after an alp of the same name in the valley below. It then descends into the Valgrisanche, follows this north and returns into France over the Col du Mont and thence to base via the Mercuel and the forests above Le Crot and Ste Foy. This seems to have been first proposed as a walk by the guides of the new ski resort of Ste Foy and is a very worthwhile expedition. The Plan du Clou and its Balmes glaciers has already been described in the introduction to the chapter.

The walk is described in the anticlockwise direction as this minimises the ascent on the first day to 1034m. In the other direction the ascent is 865m to the Col du Mont and another 484m up the Valgrisanche, which makes a hard day. Only one night in a refuge is needed but a second can be had at La Motte in the Mercuel if you wish to shorten the stages in either direction. Passports are essential as they will be needed by the guardian in the Refuge Bezzi

Approach: Drive along the Tarentaise Valley to Ste Foy la Thuile where a road leaves on the left if driving up the valley, signposted to Ste Foy Station. Follow this to the new ski resort, eventually passing near a chair-lift on the left. There is parking and the walk can be started here. It is probably better, though, to continue past the hamlet of Bon Conseil, which is just ahead of you, and follow a track for about 3km which leads through woods to a parking area where there is a "no entry" sign. Park here. The track is rough but presents no real difficulties.

First day: Destination the Refuge Mario Bezzi via the Col du Rocher Blanc (2833m)

Time needed: 4h 50min to the col. Descent to the refuge will take a good 1¹/₂h.

Height gain: 1034m

Ascent: Continue along the track, which ascends a little, then becomes level and passes the hamlet of l'Echaillon and so to Le Monal through colourful pastures with magnificent views across the trough of the Isère to the glaciers of Mt Pourri and the Dôme de la Sache. Le Monal is very attractive. Only the property owners there are allowed to take their cars and, as a result, the hamlet is remarkably tranquil. It gives a good idea of how a Savoyard hamlet might have looked in the last century. The walk so far is not demanding and makes a very pleasant day out for a young family. There is also a refuge at Le Monal.

Continue along the track straight through Le Monal and take a path to the left which climbs the hillside. There are two, one which goes up an open slope and one which goes entirely through the woods. The two meet and climb through woods where *Clematis alpina* grows, a plant whose flowers are not easy to see as they are an ashen blue and favour the gloom of the undergrowth. The path emerges onto open hillside and climbs to a steep track which is followed left over a little prow and then up to the summit of a ridge which bars the mouth of the Plan du Clou. The track now descends

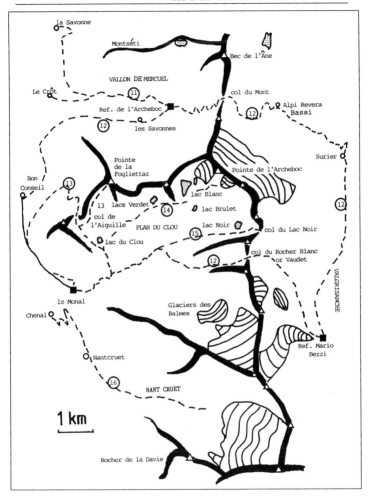

MAP 24. The mountains around the Vallon de Mercuel, the Plan du Clou and the Nant Cruet. The Valgrisanche runs south to north on the eastern side of the frontier ridge. The lines taken by walk Nos. 11 to 16 are shown

The hamlet of Le Monal

a little onto the floor of the valley and crosses the plain to a bridge and thence to the chalets of les Balmes on the slopes ahead. Cheese can be bought here in the summer. Below the chalets is a signpost to the Col du Rocher Blanc but I find it best to continue to above the chalets to a second signpost (to the Col du Lac Noir) and go right here on a less well marked path which takes you round the end of a ridge onto its southern side, with excellent views across to the glaciers of les Balmes. You soon reach undulating terrain where the path becomes less distinct though the route is clear enough and makes for a V-shaped gap ahead which is passed using a path on its left slope. Note the green, serpentine rocks to the right of this trough. The final and steep ascent to the col follows, fortunately not too prolonged, and you can see at last the mountains across the Valgrisanche.

Continue down fairly steep slopes with only a faint path, into the bottom of the Grapillon Valley below. The terrain is mainly scree and is the home of thousands of plants of *Linaria alpina*. It is best to keep to the left of the valley and make for an obvious footpath below, which comes into the Grapillon from the left over a lower ridge. This is the way up to the Col du Lac Noir from the Valgrisanche. Join this path and follow it to the right to the end of the valley which is very dramatically cut away where it hangs over the Valgrisanche. The path crosses the stream and makes a descending traverse right along the wall of the Valgrisanche. It follows steep grassy slopes suspended between lines of crag above and below - a path to be taken with respect. It is also necessary to cross a couple of glacier streams. The refuge can be seen below long before arrival. There is a splendid view up the Valgrisanche to the Glacier de Gliarettaz. On the crest, to the left of this, is a glacier crossing back to the Tarentaise over the Col du Rhêmes-Golette. The summits of the frontier ridge above are hidden by the steepness of the rock walls of the valleyside. The peaks across the valley to the east, however, form a magnificent background. They are all well over 3000m in altitude, culminating in the Grande Rousse at 3607m.

Just before you arrive at the refuge, it is necessary to cross an eroded glacier stream on what was, in August 1992, a narrow beam which provided a test of gymnastic ability, not too welcome at the end of the day. There is then a good bridge over the main river and you are soon at the refuge. Looking back at the line of the path you have just taken, you will see above you the snout of the glacier which produces the stream with the beam bridge. This is not much more than 100m above you and is the end of the Glacier des Plattes des Chamois whose ice flows steeply down from the crest of the frontier ridge, which is some 1200m higher.

Second day: Objective, the Col du Mont and return to the starting point

Time needed: 5h 20min to the Col du Mont for a descent of 484m followed by an ascent of 839m. Allow a good hour to La Motte and it is then $7^1/_2$km to Bon Conseil, which will take somewhat over 2h. The day will thus extend to some 8h of walking. If needed this can be split into two by staying at the refuge of La Motte.

Return: Leave the refuge by the obvious path which descends north into the trough of the Valgrisanche. This descends steeply to the point near a cable lift which has been set up to provision the refuge.

From there a good track follows the valley down, past a junction which goes off to the right, and takes a left fork over a deep gorge and past the hamlet of Surier. A path on the left is marked as leading to the Col du Mont and is indeed one possible route which follows the valley bottom with no apparent difficulty. We, however, for no particular reason, followed the line of the high level path, Via Alta 4, which follows the track across the stream over an even more impressive gorge and at the second hairpin bend takes a path that cuts out much of the road, though it is overgrown in parts and is not always easy to follow exactly. The path comes back to the track at Grand Alpage and then climbs parallel with the river. The alternative path can be seen below. The Via Alta route may have a slight edge over this lower path since height is gained more easily. The track arrives at the buildings and manure store of Alpi Revera Bassi and peters out into a path which passes the buildings on the left. The path forks shortly afterwards, the right-hand going to the Lago di San Grato and the left, which you take, to the col. The path descends a little to a bridge and then makes an ascending traverse to the left towards a ridge which it climbs in a series of zig-zags. The slope eases and the path passes a ruined building not marked on the maps, then climbs more steeply over rocky terrain before arriving at the Col du Mont.

From the col, descend towards La Motte using the path which leads off to the left. From a little above the hamlet, a path will be observed in the distance across some hay meadows to the left, which climbs a small bank and passes beside a small circular lake. Cross to this path, avoiding the hay, and follow it to Les Savonnes (do not confuse with La Savonne), a group of chalets beside a stream. The path continues beside a low wall and traverses first through bilberry wire and then forest. It is always clear and is marked by occasional red splashes of paint. Eventually, a turning point at the end of a forest track is reached. The track descends regularly through the forest and occasional views are obtained across and down to Le Crot. Leave the track at the first real right-hand hairpin bend on a path which leads to Le Planay Dessous and so Le Planay Dessus. Here take the central route through the village onto a pleasant green lane which takes you through open country to a road a little below Bon Conseil. From there rejoin the car. There is a small restaurant near the start of the chair-lift, which could prove popular.

Summary of refuges

Du Monal - Altitude 1874m. Meals provided. Closed in the spring. 20 beds (79 06 94 17 for information and booking). Private.

Mario Bezzi - Altitude 2284m. Meals provided. Open 1/7 to 30/9. 40 beds, mostly in small rooms. Run by CAI Turin. French spoken and French francs accepted in payment; allow around 40,000 lire per person for excellent dinner, bed and breakfast, (1992 prices) (19-39 165 97129).

La Motte - Altitude 2080m. Meals provided. Open 1/6 to 15/9. 36 beds (79 09 51 31 - radio link). Recently renamed the Refuge de l'Archeboc.

13: Col de l'Aiguille and Pointe de la Foglietta (2930m)

Grade:	2 to col, 4 to summit of the Foglietta
Map:	3532ET
Time needed:	2h 30min to col or 3h 50min to pointe
Height gain:	1132m
Comment:	The north side of the Col de l'Aiguille used to be a very pleasant walk though it has been modified to improve the ski piste for the new ski resort of Ste Foy and a chair-lift has been constructed to a point east of the col. The walk remains, if not as pleasant as before. The walk starts through woods, then over an open, floriferous hillside to the col and returns via the Plan du Clou and Le Monal

Approach: Park in the area on the track to Le Monal as described for Walk No.12.

Ascent: Set out in the direction of Le Monal but after only a few yards take a path which turns off sharp left and takes a climbing traverse above the car park. Keep left at the junction of the path from L'Echaillon. A clearing in the woods is reached with a path coming up from the left. Continue up a short, steep bank to meet the track which climbs from Plan Bois and follow this to the chalets of L'Arpettaz. Climb above the chalets and find a path which climbs steeply up the hillside on your right. The path keeps generally to the left of the combe above to avoid steep precipitous ground and eventually traverses right to the col where there is a small wooden chalet. There are three possibilities from the col:

1) Go to the right and climb the Arbine (2647m) by the obvious path near the ridge. Descend via the rocky ridge overlooking Lac du Clou, avoiding moving too far left. The ground is not difficult but broken and rocky and requires some sense of navigation. The rocks are remarkably crevassed. Aim to descend to the left a little below Lac du Clou to rejoin the path marked on the map.

2) To ascend the Foglietta, descend a little and traverse left into the combe which leads towards the summit. A cross on the ridge is reached easily and is called the Croix de Foglietta. The summit is reached over rocks which are at an easy angle but which are loose and require care, the sort of rocks where it is inadvisable to pull strongly on the holds. The summit is well worthwhile and gives splendid views of the surrounding mountains and of the Tarentaise Valley.

Descent: By the same route to join the path from the col.

3) **Descent:** Simply continue down from the col over easy ground with some aid from footpaths, passing either side of Lac du Clou but then tending right to pass the chalets of Le Clou. Here join a track which crosses a bridge by a small dam. Immediately afterwards, cut off to the right up a path which climbs to the top of the ridge barring entry to the Plan du Clou. From here follow the route down to Le Monal and the car park as described in reverse for Walk No.12.

14: Pointe d'Archeboc (3272m)

Grade: 4
Map: 3532ET
Time needed: 5h 20min
Height gain: 1473m

Comment: A demanding walk up a high mountain with little in the way of paths to help on the upper slopes. An excellent viewpoint.

Approach: Start from the parking place on the track to Le Monal as described for Walk No.12.

Ascent: Climb to the Plan du Clou (Walk No.12) and descend and cross the river to the hamlets of Le Clou (Walk No.13). Climb towards Lac du Clou but before reaching this strike out to the right along a vague ledge in the hillside, using the ground to make height and arrive at the outlet to Lacs Verdet. Continue from the lake and climb a little ridge which falls from the Pointe de l'Argentière until Lac Blanc comes into view. Follow a level boulder field without descending to the lake until a path is found which climbs up on the right of a rocky ridge. This turns into an open gully which may be either bare scree or névé, depending on the time of year and season. This slope leads to much gentler ground, about half way between the summits of the Archeboc and Ormelune, which is in fact a small glacier, the Glacier d'Archeboc. This provides no problem even if

The Testa del Rutor from the Archeboc with the Lago dí San Grato cradled below its cliffs

bare ice, since the surface will be rough and the crevasses are small. Climb it to the ridge separating the two summits and climb left to the Archeboc over screes and easy rock. There is a spacious summit with very open views both of the Italian mountains and of the Montséti and its Lac Noir, the Lago di San Grato, the Testa del Rutor, the Aiguille de la Grande Sassière, Mt Pourri and many others.

Descent: By the route used for the ascent. It is, in fact, possible to descend to Lac Brulet and towards the head of the valley near Lac Noir but this involves steep and broken ground full of traps for the unwary. This would be feasible for an experienced and confident party but it is not possible to describe in any useful way.

15: Lac Noir and its col (2869m)

Grade:	2 to lac, 3 to col
Map:	3532ET
Time needed:	3h 10min to lake, 4h 5min to col
Height gain:	819m to lake, 1070 to col
Comment:	Another walk in the valley of the Plan du Clou which is less demanding than the previous one but which takes the walker into a very wild corner of the valley. The lake is magnificently situated in the hollow of a deep and rocky combe

Approach: Start from the parking place on the track to Le Monal as described in Walk No.12.

Ascent: Climb to the Plan du Clou and so to the chalets of les Balmes as for the start of Walk No.12. Above the chalets, continue left along the path signposted to Lac Noir. This tends to keep above the valley bottom with the stream to the left, though it is eventually possible to descend to the stream and follow this to the lake. In order to reach the col, a path is followed which climbs above the lake, still keeping this on the left. This is stopped by a tongue of loose scree, which it is necessary to surmount, then follow the shallow valley behind to the col. Considerable accumulations of snow may be present just below the col.

Descent: By the same route. A pleasant variation is also possible. As you descend with the lake a little way behind, a grassy plateau will be observed on the left which leads to the top of the ridge separating the Lac Noir valley from the moraines of the Glaciers des Balmes. It is easy to follow this route, even though there is no path, and descend a little the other side of the ridge to pick up a path which leads down to the chalets of les Balmes.

16: The Nant Cruet

Grade:	3
Map:	3532ET
Time needed:	2h 40min
Height gain:	About 800m
Comment:	A pleasant walk on track and path which leads finally into a superb glacier cirque

Approach: Drive along the main valley to Les Pigettes, a hamlet which is reached just before the road passes beneath avalanche protection roofs (if driving up the valley). Turn sharp left here and climb a narrow, surfaced road to a car park at Chenal.

Ascent: The road from here climbs to Le Monal and also gives access to the road up to the Plan du Clou. For the present walk, climb a little way and take the right fork in the direction of the hamlet of Nantcruet, through the summer meadows. The track continues after the hamlet and leads into the valley of the Nant Cruet to a water collection point. From there a path keeps to the left of the stream and high above it and climbs open ground making for a V-shaped opening in the valley ahead. There is little path here but once through the gap you emerge into an open bowl overhung by the Glaciers du Fond and de la Sassière, the latter falling from the Aiguille de la Grande Sassière, one of the highest mountains in the region. The name, of course, has nothing to do with the hamlet of the same name further north.

Descent: By the same route.

SOME SHORT WALKS

1. **From Séez** - In the centre of the village, above the Mairie, there

is a signpost directing you to St Germain, Le Mont and VR (Voie Romaine, the old Roman road over the Col du Petit St Bernard). Follow this track on foot up the hillside and go left where it meets another track. This takes you round into the ravine of the river Le Reclus and to a wide bridge across the river. Cross this and climb steeply for a short way then a path will be seen turning sharply to the left and marked by a yellow blob of paint on a rock. Climb this to its junction with another path and go right. The new path climbs steadily but at a reasonable angle. A junction is reached after a short distance, signposted left to Le Mont (Le Mont Villaret on the map) or straight on to St Germain. The path to Le Mont climbs steep zig-zags and gives a brisk climb. We will, however, continue gently towards St Germain through woods, then across open hillside to a road. Go left to St Germain where there is a chapel, a restored watermill and picnic tables. - (*Grade 1*, ascent 357m.)

The road forks here, the left one going to Le Mont whence you can return via the steep path already mentioned, which turns off just by the lower houses. Or go on to Le Cottier and down through the forest, which is pleasant on a hot day. The right fork at St Germain takes you onto the lower slopes of the Aiguille du Clapet and the old Roman road, though this is a longer walk. Or go back down the road to Séez.

At Villard Dessus above Séez there is a large, barrack-like building on the right with parking across the road. A track passes in front of this and becomes a path which goes straight on in the direction of the hamlet of Le Noyeray, coming down to the road between some old chalets. Cross the road and descend to the hamlet and take a lane which goes down among the houses and turns left. There are some interesting house decorations here. Continue onto a path which traverses the hillside and go down at the first junction. This follows a small stream to some buildings not marked on the map and where a track will return you to Le Breuil and thence, by side road, to the car. - (*Grade 1*, total height gain 150m.)

2. **Plan Bois** - This is a very pleasant picnic spot and is reached by driving to Bon Conseil above Ste Foy and on to Le Monal (Walk No.12). A left turning is reached which is signposted to Plan Bois. The car can be left here as the road higher up is rough. Follow the track for about 1km until it forks and take the right-hand, rising

branch which leads quickly to open meadows with attractive views. - (*Grade 1.*) The walk can be extended by parking near Bon Conseil and walking from there. If this option is taken you can return by using a track which descends from near the fork, through woods to the chapel just the other side of Bon Conseil.

3. **Already described** - La Savonne and the Jourdan Valley with the river and its pools among flowery meadows (Walk No.7, *Grade 1*). A longer but delightful outing is to walk from La Savonne into the Vallon de Mercuel (Walk No.11, *Grade 2*). Le Monal is well worth a visit (Walk No.12, *Grade 1*) and several walks start there. One starts by the refuge and is signposted to La Combaz. This descends through meadows to the hamlet and there becomes a track which descends in the direction of Chenal. Turn left where this joins another track and return to Le Monal via Le Fenil, keeping left at the next fork - (*Grade 2*). To return to the car park, go north in the centre of Le Monal, through a group of chalets and over a bridge across the stream that flows down from the Plan du Clou. Follow a more or less well marked path through woods and clearings down to the stream and then along the edge of a meadow to meet the track to the car park where this crosses the stream.

4. **The hamlets of Montvalezan** - This recently inaugurated walk starts at the village of Montvalezan (Map 21) and climbs the hillside using entirely tracks, only touching the roads occasionally. There is a map in the village showing the route, which is marked by yellow arrows and signposts. Start either in the village or at a parking place some 300m west. Climb through the hamlets of Solliet, Les Laix and Pré du Four to Hauteville, where you do not go up to the road but descend on a track to La Combaz, then the road to Le Châtelard with its white church on a rocky knoll. The "official" route then takes you to Le Vaz and back on the road, though there is an attractive and shorter alternative. From behind the church, a path goes east and curves around the knoll to the right, then zig-zags down to the road. Cross this and descend via the interesting church of Notre Dame de Liesse, more or less directly to Montvalezan. Much of this route is marked in red on map 3532ET but there are some differences. The walk involves some 400m of ascent and you should allow 2h 10min minimum. A charming walk through some very attractive hamlets. I class this *Grade 2* because of the amount of climbing involved.

CHAPTER 6

Around Val d'Isère

INTRODUCTION

Here we are almost at the end of the Tarentaise valleys. Val, as it is known to skiers, is a major winter sports centre with much development around an original old village. There is, as one would expect, a large concentration of ski uplift equipment but this covers a remarkably small proportion of the mountains around and there is a great deal of unspoiled countryside. Nor is Val a dead end since the Tarentaise and Maurienne valleys are connected here by the Col de l'Iseran which in summer tempts motorists in their thousands to negotiate its hairpin bends and high summit. The eastern extremity of the Vanoise National Park forms a belt around the south and east of the village and there is a nature reserve to the north so that it makes a very good walking centre. The frontier with Italy also swings around the head of the valley, and while there are no easy crossings in this region, the mountains exceed 3000m in altitude and provide a very impressive backdrop to the walks that I shall describe. There are two big lakes: Lac du Chevril just below Val and Lac de la Sassière nestled under the southern wall of the Aiguille de la Grande Sassière. Both are man-made, part of the hydro-electric system.

The area is fully covered by the D&R map No.11 or by two TOP25 maps, 3633ET - Tignes, Val d'Isère, Haute Maurienne and 3532ET - Les Arcs, La Plagne.

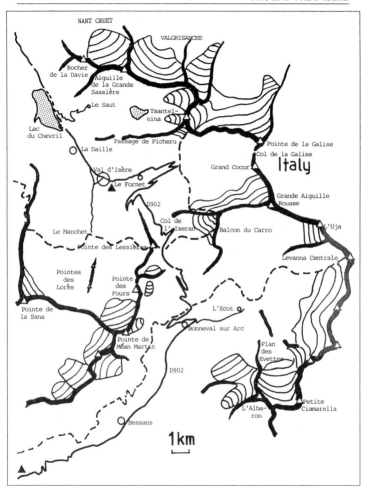

MAP 25. The region described in Chapter 6 showing the road connecting the Tarentaise with the Maurienne via the Col de l'Iseran and the minor roads used for access. The layout of the ridges separating France and Italy and separating Tarentaise and Maurienne are also shown. The dashed line follows the boundary of the Vanoise National Park

185

1: Rocher de la Davie (3156m)

Grade:	3 but steep in part
Map:	3532ET
Time needed:	3h 15min
Height gain:	876m
Comment:	A summit which gives a close view of the Aiguille de la Grande Sassière and a panorama of the hills to the south of Val d'Isère. It is situated on the ridge between the Nant Cruet and Lac du Chevril

Approach: Drive along the Lac du Chevril. About half way along, between two tunnels, there is a turn off on the side opposite the lake, signposted to the Villaret du Nial. Follow this road which climbs the hillside in a series of hairpins and then turns into the mouth of a rocky side valley and leads quite quickly to a parking place below a small dam at a place called Le Saut. Note that this is a very popular venue and can be packed with cars later in the day.

Ascent: The valley ahead is dominated by the 1500m wall of the Grande Sassière. You turn left away from this and follow a gently rising path to and behind the chalets at Le Chargeur and continue around the hillside. As the path climbs, a disused water conduit will be noticed running parallel with the path. Eventually this swings away right and is shadowed by another path which leads up into the Grande Combe. The square cairn on the summit of the Rocher de la Davie is visible from here and the pale rocks of the Rocher Blanc below, to the left. It is now necessary to cross the ridge below the Rocher Blanc, which involves much boulder hopping over large blocks. Keep below the lowest cliffs on this ridge. This brings you round into a flat bottomed combe with a little col visible on its far side. A ridge that is half scree, half grass rises to the right from this col and can be climbed from the col, which is much frequented by sheep and is deep in their droppings. (I am told that these animals are brought up for the summer grazing from the South of France.) However, above and on the right there is a higher little combe mostly cut off by a line of cliffs. Climb up on the right and find sheep trods which lead without difficulty into this second combe. A path

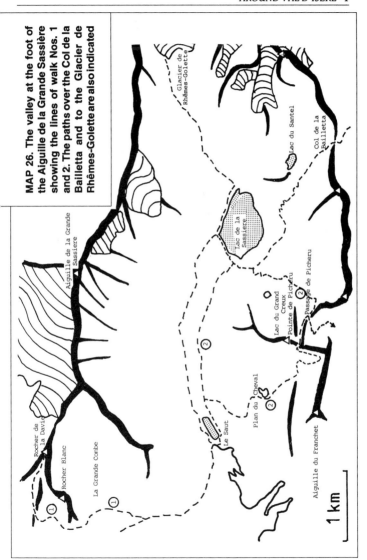

MAP 26. The valley at the foot of the Aiguille de la Grande Sassière showing the lines of walk Nos. 1 and 2. The paths over the Col de la Bailletta and to the Glacier de Rhêmes-Golette are also indicated

rising to the left will then become evident which leads to the ridge from the col and meets this half way up, so avoiding some of the steepest ground.

Continue up the ridge until you come onto the broad back of the mountain by a small cairn. Go right and make for the summit cairn, finding a path on its right for the last few metres. The summit is quite a surprise after the unsensational approach as the two cliffs which bound the mountain's back meet here and you find yourself on a narrow ridge which falls away steeply on three sides. You have a good view down to the glaciers at the head of the Nant Cruet but the view north is hidden by the wall of the Pointe des Plates de Chamois.

Descent: By the same route. It is possible to avoid the boulder hopping by following sheep trods out of the lower combe and descend to the path evident below and which takes you back directly to Le Saut.

Variation: Several footpaths are marked which traverse the hillside between Le Saut and the hamlet of Nantcruet. These can be used to extend the walk or as another, though longer approach to the mountain. I have not covered the whole of these paths but warn that the one shown traversing above Nantcruet to Le Fenil was very indefinite when I attempted to follow it some years ago.

2: Barrage de la Sassière, Passage de Picheru and Plan du Cheval

Grade:	3
Map:	3532ET
Time needed:	3h 15min for circuit
Height gain:	530m
Comment:	This is quite a short circuit but which reaches an altitude of near 2810m. It starts as a simple walk up a gently sloping valley, then a steep pull to the Passage and finally a descent over scree without paths into the pleasant bowl of the Plan du Cheval. You are also in the company of two of the higher mountains of the Tarentaise. Several other walks are possible and these will be mentioned

Approach: As for Walk No.1.

Ascent: Cross the stream below the lake and follow a path along the other side of the lake below some small cliffs. The path follows the line of the valley, rising slowly, with the dark wall of the Aiguille de la Grande Sassière on the left and the glaciers of the Tsanteleina ahead. This is a good place to observe marmots, particularly if you are there early in the morning. Just before the Lac de la Sassière the path divides, the left-hand branch going to the dam. The other branch joins a track which is followed until a narrow path is seen which strikes up the hillside on the right. This climbs steadily, then steeply until you reach a level place with views down the other side of the mountain and which is the Passage de Picheru. Note that you do not arrive at a true col as the lowest point on this ridge is below you on the left.

From here a path descends almost 1000m to La Daille. We will keep high and take to a grassy ridge (on the right as you came up to the Passage) which leads to a little gap just below the Pointe de Picheru where there is a marker post. From this gap go left and descend the ridge following a trace of a path until the way is blocked by a large gendarme. Descend slightly to the right and cross some big scree to join a path which comes down the rock slabs ahead. This is the climber's way off the Aiguille de Franchet. Descend directly with the rocks of the Franchet on the left and follow the path right as it swings around the head of a small valley and onto a broad grass ridge. Follow this down to a col where there is a fine view of the end of the Franchet. The paths fade out about here but the ground is now easy. Go right and descend to the Lac du Plan du Cheval, an attractive spot though not well known.

To continue, follow a narrow path down on the left which crosses open, alpine moorland and drops quite quickly to a wide, grassy ledge. A line of small cliffs lies below this ledge which we passed in the morning and which cut the direct route back to Le Saut. An obvious path goes straight over the edge and follows a series of little scrambles down a weak spot in the cliffs, including a step around an airy corner, back to Le Saut. Alternatively, follow a path right which takes you around the end of the cliffs and so onto the path followed on the way out.

Other Walks: Set out as described above but go to the dam and cross this on a track. You can then turn left and return down the other side of the valley (allow 1h 40min) or turn right and follow the path to the edge of the Glacier de Rhêmes-Golette (allow 1¹/₂h from the dam). At the top of this glacier is a mountaineers' col which leads to the head of the Valgrisanche and the Refuge Mario Bezzi (Walk No.14 in Chapter 5).

If you continue along the track where the turn off for the Passage de Picheru is made, you come to the Col de la Bailletta which leads to Val d'Isère. The circuit Val-Bailletta-Picheru-Val is very popular but I have not so far done this.

3: Refuge de Prariond, Col de la Galise (2987m) and Grand Cocor (3034m)

Grade:	Mostly 3 but 4 for the last part if conditions dictate that the glacier has to be crossed to reach the col
Map:	3633ET
Time needed:	1h to Prariond, 3¹/₂h to col
Height gain:	978m
Comment:	This is a very popular walk as far as the Refuge de Prariond, through the impressive Malpasset Gorge on a good but exposed path, then across lush meadows. The climb to the col leads you into much more austere mountain country

Approach: Drive from Val d'Isère towards the Col de l'Iseran. Just before the road really starts to climb, it makes a wide right-hand bend across a bridge, the Pont St Charles. There is a big car park just before the bridge.

Ascent: A well marked path starts at the car park and quickly makes height, then levels out and makes for an obvious gorge, the Gorge du Malpasset. The path meanders along the wall of the gorge in an impressive position, and though exposed is also wide and secure. As it exits from the gorge, the path drops a little to the Prariond meadows where marmots pose for photographs. The path crosses the meadows to the refuge where refreshments are available.

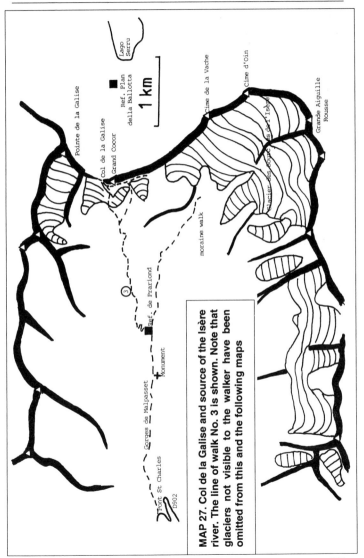

MAP 27. Col de la Galise and source of the Isère river. The line of walk No. 3 is shown. Note that glaciers not visible to the walker have been omitted from this and the following maps

From the Pointe des Lessières with the Aiguille de la Grande Sassière behind

About half way to the refuge is a memorial to some British and Italian soldiers who lost their lives hereabouts towards the end of the 1939-45 war. Their story is told in the book *Alpine Partisan* (V. Milroy, Hammond, Hammond & Co, London, 1957) by one of the two survivors, Alfred Southon. Italian partisans and escaped British prisoners of war decided to join up with the French resistance which was strong in Savoie. They crossed the Col de la Galise on the 7th November 1944 but were overtaken by a blizzard which raged for six days. They were not particularly well equipped and perished on the French side of the col, not all that far from safety.

The path zig-zags up the hillside behind the refuge, following the line of a stream with attractive waterfalls. It leaves the stream to follow the line of a ridge but it is well worth deviating from this and following the stream further as there are often groups of male bouquetin to be found here. They can be approached quite closely but remember that it is forbidden to disturb the animals in the National Park. Climb up on the right to regain the path and follow this over increasingly rocky ground, making for the right of the col. Climb to a path which traverses into the col. If there is much névé it may be necessary to traverse across snow, though there is usually a beaten path to help you. The col is quite spacious and there is a magnificent view down into the Italian valley. There is also another memorial.

To reach the Grand Cocor, follow the path to the right on the French side of the ridge and you will reach the rounded summit in a few minutes.

Descent: By the same route. It is possible to continue for a short way from the Grand Cocor and descend from the ridge on a scree path on the right.

Alternative: If you do not wish to go as high as the Col de la Galise, continue up the valley past the refuge over a moraine full of flowers. Ahead is the glacier of the Sources de l'Isère with the Grande Aiguille Rousse behind.

4: Pointe des Lessières (3043m)

Grade:	4
Map:	3633ET
Time needed:	1h 15min
Height gain:	369m
Comment:	A short ascent but by no means easy. Best avoided early in the season or if the route is much covered by snow. A good viewpoint

Approach: Drive to the top of the Col de l'Iseran where there is parking to left and to right and much tourism.

Ascent: The Lessières is the sharp peak south-west of the col and clearly visible. It is high but the approach via the col means a relatively modest ascent. Make for the foot of the evident ridge on the left of the peak as seen from the col. Several paths climb scree to reach a path which wends its way, more or less following the ridge and which has some quite airy passages. A short section with a fixed rope is encountered first and, near the top, a short scramble is necessary up a groove to the ridge on the left. The summit is quite commodious.

Descent: By the same route.

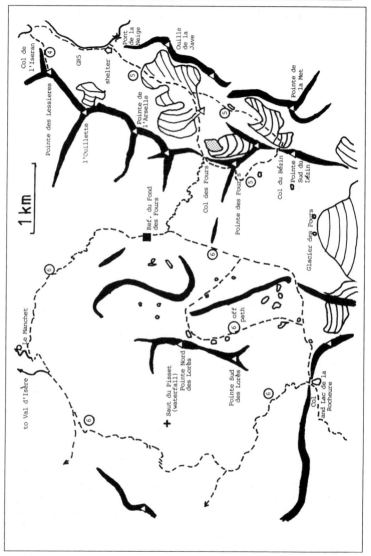

5: Pointe des Fours (3072m) and Col de Bézin

Grade: 4
Map: 3633ET
Time needed: 1h 50min to Pointe, 2h for the return descent
Height gain: 690m
Comment: A short and very pleasant walk to high altitude with excellent views of the hills to the south of Val d'Isère. You are certain to encounter névé

Approach: About 2^1/$_2$km south of the Col de l'Iseran is a road bridge called Pont de la Neige with plenty of parking nearby. For a party without transport, it may be possible to use the cable-car and telecabin system which takes people up for the summer skiing from Le Fornet. Check, of course, whether this is operating. Walk from the col to Pont de la Neige using the G.R.5 footpath.

Ascent: There is a shelter beside the road and a path climbs from near this into the valley above, whose end is not visible from the road. The slope eases after a while and the path takes to névé in the raised centre of the valley. There is usually a well beaten path in the snow. There are two cols at the head of the valley. Make directly for the snow slope below them and tend towards the right-hand col. Climb to this, then traverse over the slope on the right, above a lake, to the Col des Fours. There may also be some névé on this traverse. Climb to the Pointe des Fours on the west facing side of the ridge above the col.

From the Pointe a broken ridge falls to the west into the Vallon des Fours. Descend this until it is possible to traverse left (looking down) on fine, flaky scree to the Col de Bézin which is clearly visible.

MAP 28 (on facing page). The region immediately south of Val d'Isère and within the National Park. The lines of walk Nos. 4, 5 and 6 are shown including the off-path variation of the latter, as is the path connecting walk Nos. 5 and 6 on the western slopes of the Col des Fours. The two arrowed paths at the western extreme of the map make a loup around the Croix du Pisset, which is not described in the text. The path going south-west from the Col de la Rocheure leads to the Refuge de la Femma and Termignon

There is likely to be a cornice in the snow on the other side of the col and it will probably be best to go to the right to avoid this. Descend where the angle and conditions are safe and follow the valley down to a little lake whose outlet stream almost overhangs the lower Iseran road. Climb straight ahead to a col which is the left-hand one of the two you approached on the ascent. Avoid climbing on snow, if possible, since by the time you arrive at this point it is likely to be soft and laborious to climb. From the col descend by the route of ascent.

Descent: If you do not wish to cross the Col de Bézin, return by the route used for the ascent to the Pointe des Fours.

Alternatives: For those who have used the cable-cars from the Fornet, the quickest way back to Val d'Isère is to descend the path on the west side of the Col des Fours to the Refuge du Fond des Fours and thence down to Le Manchet and the road back to Val.

6: Circuit des Pointes des Lorès

Grade:	3
Map:	3633ET
Time needed:	Conventional route 5½h; variation 6h
Height gain:	950m
Comment:	This circuit follows paths which lead to the Col de la Rocheure, a high col from where it is possible to descend towards the Maurienne. The pivotal point is a ridge running north-south with the two summits of the Lorès, which are hardly any higher than the maximum reached on the tour. The walk covers a large tract of stony moorland and remains at high altitude for an extended distance. The scenery seems rather austere but is relieved by small lakes and, in August, by the brilliant splashes of colour of scree-dwelling alpine plants.
	We will describe the tour in the clockwise direction though it can be done either way

Approach: Drive from Val d'Isère, south to Le Manchet. The road crosses to the eastern bank of the stream and passes a sports area. At Le Manchet it becomes a track and climbs to large parking areas.

Ascent: Continue up the track, then path to the Refuge du Fond des Fours. The ascent is steep at times but the path is good. From beside the refuge a little col is visible almost straight ahead. Continue on the path but where this strikes uphill towards the Col des Fours, keep straight on across a small plain, then steeply up to the near col from which you look down on the morain of the Glacier des Fours. Here it is necessary to choose which route we are to take.

Conventional route: The right-hand side of the valley is lined with cliffs, and about a mile away there is a small bluff, beneath the cliff and beside the morain. Make in its direction and pass it on its left. A cairned path will be found making a rising traverse of the scree beyond and which climbs to a gap in the cliffs with close views of the Pointe de la Méan Martin. The path climbs through rocks, then descends a little below the Col du Pisset and climbs again finally to traverse a steep scree slope to the Col de la Rocheure. Névé is likely to be encountered, particularly early in the season. The col gives a good view of the ridge to the south which separates you from the valley of the Maurienne and of the Glacier de la Vanoise over to the right, all set off by the lake just below you on the south side of the col.

Descend a steep and narrow path over scree to the north and follow the excellent path which leads steadily down to the track which returns to Le Manchet. At just after the half way mark this traverses steep grass and then descends in zig-zags towards the river again, making an excellent grandstand to view the parallel waterfalls of the Saut du Pisset. The track to Le Manchet is followed for a while to a signpost which advises you to cross the river (bridge) and climb a little bump before the final descent to the car. This avoids the quarrying operations which have rather defaced the lower part of the track.

Off-path variation: From the col above the Refuge du Fond des Fours a line of low cliffs will be seen inclining up to the right and above which is a break in the main cliffs. Make for the lowest, left-hand part of this band of rock and climb grassy slopes behind until you are looking down into a small bowl. This should be crossed, either across its bottom or by boulder hopping over blocks on the left, and the grassy slopes on the other side climbed until it is possible to turn left around the end of the upper cliffs. Aim more or less for the Pointe Nord des Lorès to reach a little tarn nestled at the foot of its screes. Now climb left onto a shelf and walk parallel with the Lorès ridge, passing two more tarns. You may be lucky to find edelweiss here (remember all flora is protected in the National Park) and certainly *Aster alpinus,* deep red *Saxifraga oppositifolia* and an abundance of slate blue *Campanula cenisia.* A ridge ahead drops from the Pointe Sud des Lorès; go round to the left of this, following a little valley in a southerly direction, climbing eventually to meet the path already described for the conventional route, prior to the traverse to the Col de la Rocheure.

Note that this relatively level area that you traverse will have an extensive snow cover early in the season so that this variant to the tour is probably best done in the August/September period. There are, in fact, many tarns nestled in the folds of this high moorland which add to its scenic value but which will be under snow early in the season - another reason for leaving this walk till the snow has melted.

7: Balcon du Carro

Grade:	2
Map:	3633ET
Time needed:	6¹/₂h for the return trip
Height gain:	On outward leg 580m
Comment:	This is a long walk of some 20km there and back but with relatively little climbing, most of it in the first 2km. Since the walk ends at a refuge there are refreshments in view for those in need. At the same time the walk provides a magnificent and continuous spectacle of the big peaks which form the Franco-Italian frontier; a cirque of peaks around the head of the Maurienne Valley, almost all over 3300m in altitude and all heavily glaciated

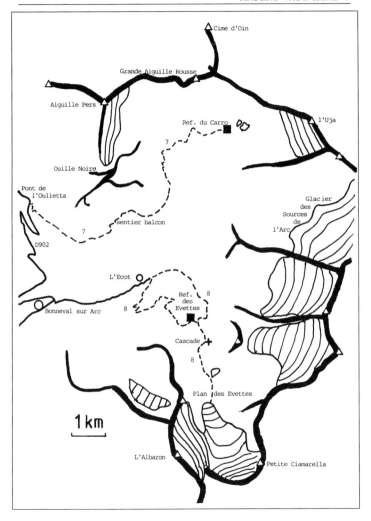

MAP 29. The cirque within which rises the Arc river, south of the Col de l'Iseran. The lines taken by walk Nos. 7 and 8 are shown, the eastern loup of 8 being the Sentier à John

199

Approach: From the top of the Col de l'Iseran, drive in the direction of Bonneval sur Arc, past the Pont de la Neige and through a gorge and tunnel to a parking place at the Pont de l'Oulietta. Altitude 2476m.

Ascent: An obvious path climbs the hillside to the east of the road and gains height steadily until it reaches about 2700m when it traverses gently this great elevated balcony. It starts to descend and swing around the pivot of the Ouille des Reys where there is danger, for a short distance, of stones rolling down the screes above. The danger is slight *provided* you do not linger. The path then crosses a wide, grassy bowl and climbs gently to the Refuge du Carro and its black and white lakes.

Return: By the same route.

8: Plan des Evettes (2590m)

Grade:	2 or by the Sentier à John, 4
Map:	3633ET
Time needed:	2h 20min to foot of Glacier des Evettes
Height gain:	560m
Comment:	An easy walk which takes you right into the heart of a magnificent glacier cirque, with the added bonus of a close look at a splendid waterfall with rainbow in its spray

Approach: Drive to Bonneval sur Arc where the main road makes a wide, almost 180 degree turn as it attacks the climb to the Col de l'Iseran. A road goes off the outside of this bend and one branch goes immediately right and crosses the river. This is followed up the valley as far as a car park opposite the hamlet of L'Écot. This hamlet was, not so long ago, in ruins and has been very sympathetically restored in the manner traditional for the region.

Ascent: A path leaves the parking place in a south-westerly direction and makes a steady climbing traverse of the hillside. After a couple of changes in direction you are led into a shallow, sloping valley which, if followed to its end, brings you onto the morain plain of the Plan des Evettes. The Refuge des Evettes is situated on a small hill above you, on the left. Make for and pass the refuge on paths which meander among rocky bluffs until you can descend to a stone bridge at the left-hand corner of the Plan des Evettes. All the melt water from the glaciers passes under this bridge and almost immediately crashes down into the gorge below, throwing up a cloud of spray in which a rainbow is formed. This is the Cascade de la Reculaz. There are several places above the gorge where it is possible to obtain a good view of the fall and photograph it.

Cross the bridge and walk onto the morain plain. It is possible to walk right up to the tongue of the Glacier des Evettes. There is also a lake which is worth a visit. The main glacier streams run to your right and are usually too full to ford.

Descent: By the route used for the ascent. Note that the short cut across the upper hairpin of the path is very eroded and is not a particularly pleasant way down.

Sentier à John: This is an exciting alternative to the ordinary route described above. It is probably best avoided in wet conditions.

From the car park, continue in the direction of the main valley. A track crosses a flat river plain and makes for the point where the river from the Plan des Evettes joins the Arc river. A path turns the corner on the right and follows the side valley which eventually leads to the Cascade de la Reculaz. You gain little height at first but then start to climb through rocky outcrops which involve the odd bit of scrambling. The waterfall is seen face on from a couple of vantage points, the last being a rock prow which overhangs the gorge. From this point the path goes right and climbs rapidly to a little gully which is awkward enough to have been provided with a chain handrail for assistance. Scrambling up steep but simple rock and scree follows until you arrive at a signpost which tells you where you have been. Turn right for the refuge, left for the bridge and top of the waterfall.

Note that, atypically, this route is well provided with cairns to mark the way. It also must be stressed that the TOP25 map is quite wrong about the last part of the route: under no circumstances should you attempt to carry on up the gorge and climb the waterfall!

Descent: By the ordinary route or, if you have a head for heights, by the Sentier à John.

SOME SHORT WALKS

All the short walks suggested below are sections of the walks already described.

1. **La Grande Combe** lies below the Rocher de la Davie and is reached as described for Walk No.1. Do not, however, go around the ridge of the Rocher Blanc but continue up the stream to the level floor of the combe. A pleasant, secluded place for a picnic. Allow a good hour to get there. - *Grade 1.*

2. **The Lac de la Sassière** from Le Saut makes a pleasant round trip over well flowered prairies and is described in Walk No.2. Allow 1^1/$_2$-2h for the round trip. - *Grade 1.*

3. **Refuge de Prariond** is a very popular walk and you will not be on your own. The scenery through the Gorge du Malpasset and around the head of the valley is magnificent. The approach is described in Walk No.3. Allow about 1h to the refuge. - *Grade 2.*

4. **The Saut du Pisset** is a very fine waterfall. It is reached from Le Manchet by starting Walk No.6 in the anticlockwise direction. Allow about 1h to reach the grandstand view of the falls. - *Grade 2.*

5. **L'Écot** is an attractive hamlet near Bonneval sur Arc. Either walk from Bonneval (1h) or park as described for Walk No.8 when the hamlet is just across the river. There is a path north of the river and a road on the south side. - *Grade 1.*

CICERONE GUIDES
Cicerone publish a wide range of reliable guides to walking and climbing in Britain, and other general interest books.

LAKE DISTRICT - General Books
CONISTON COPPER A History
CHRONICLES OF MILNTHORPE
A DREAM OF EDEN
THE HIGH FELLS OF LAKELAND
LAKELAND - A taste to remember (Recipes)
LAKELAND VILLAGES
LAKELAND TOWNS
THE LOST RESORT? (Morecambe)
LOST LANCASHIRE (Furness area)
OUR CUMBRIA Stories of Cumbrian Men and Women
THE PRIORY OF CARTMEL
REFLECTIONS ON THE LAKES
AN ILLUSTRATED COMPANION INTO LAKELAND

LAKE DISTRICT - Guide Books
THE BORDERS OF LAKELAND
BIRDS OF MORECAMBE BAY
CASTLES IN CUMBRIA
CONISTON COPPER MINES Field Guide
THE CUMBRIA CYCLE WAY
THE EDEN WAY
IN SEARCH OF WESTMORLAND
SHORT WALKS IN LAKELND-1: SOUTH LAKELAND
SCRAMBLES IN SNOWDONIA
MORE SCRAMBLES IN THE LAKE DISTRICT
WALKING ROUND THE LAKES
WALKS IN SILVERDALE/ARNSIDE
WESTMORLAND HERITAGE WALK
WINTER CLIMBS IN THE LAKE DISTRICT

NORTHERN ENGLAND (outside the Lakes
BIRDWATCHING ON MERSEYSIDE
CANAL WALKS Vol 1 North
CANOEISTS GUIDE TO THE NORTH EAST
THE CLEVELAND WAY & MISSING LINK
THE DALES WAY
DOUGLAS VALLEY WAY
WALKING IN THE FOREST OF BOWLAND
HADRIANS WALL Vol 1 The Wall Walk
HERITAGE TRAILS IN NW ENGLAND
THE ISLE OF MAN COASTAL PATH
IVORY TOWERS & DRESSED STONES (Follies)
THE LANCASTER CANAL
LANCASTER CANAL WALKS
A WALKERS GUIDE TO THE LANCASTER CANAL
LAUGHS ALONG THE PENNINE WAY
A NORTHERN COAST-TO-COAST
NORTH YORK MOORS Walks
THE REIVERS WAY (Northumberland)
THE RIBBLE WAY
ROCK CLIMBS LANCASHIRE & NW
WALKING DOWN THE LUNE
WALKING IN THE SOUTH PENNINES
WALKING IN THE NORTH PENNINES
WALKING IN THE WOLDS
WALKS IN THE YORKSHIRE DALES (3 VOL)
WALKS IN LANCASHIRE WITCH COUNTRY
WALKS IN THE NORTH YORK MOORS
WALKS TO YORKSHIRE WATERFALLS (2 vol)
WATERFALL WALKS -TEESDALE & THE HIGH PENNINES
WALKS ON THE WEST PENNINE MOORS
WALKING NORTHERN RAILWAYS (2 vol)
THE YORKSHIRE DALES A walker's guide

Also a full range of EUROPEAN and OVERSEAS guidebooks - walking, long distance trails, scrambling, ice-climbing, rock climbing.

DERBYSHIRE & EAST MIDLANDS
KINDER LOG
HIGH PEAK WALKS
WHITE PEAK WAY
WHITE PEAK WALKS - 2 Vols
WEEKEND WALKS IN THE PEAK DISTRICT
THE VIKING WAY
THE DEVIL'S MILL / WHISTLING CLOUGH (Novels)

WALES & WEST MIDLANDS
ASCENT OF SNOWDON
WALKING IN CHESHIRE
CLWYD ROCK
HEREFORD & THE WYE VALLEY A Walker's Guide
HILLWALKING IN SNOWDONIA
HILL WALKING IN WALES (2 Vols)
THE MOUNTAINS OF ENGLAND & WALES Vol 1 WALES
WALKING OFFA'S DYKE PATH
THE RIDGES OF SNOWDONIA
ROCK CLIMBS IN WEST MIDLANDS
SARN HELEN Walking Roman Road
SCRAMBLES IN SNOWDONIA
SNOWDONIA WHITE WATER SEA & SURF
THE SHROPSHIRE HILLS A Walker's Guide
WALKING DOWN THE WYE
WELSH WINTER CLIMBS

SOUTH & SOUTH WEST ENGLAND
WALKING IN THE CHILTERNS
COTSWOLD WAY
COTSWOLD WALKS (3 VOLS)
WALKING ON DARTMOOR
WALKERS GUIDE TO DARTMOOR PUBS
EXMOOR & THE QUANTOCKS
THE KENNET & AVON WALK
LONDON THEME WALKS
AN OXBRIDGE WALK
A SOUTHERN COUNTIES BIKE GUIDE
THE SOUTHERN-COAST-TO-COAST
SOUTH DOWNS WAY & DOWNS LINK
SOUTH WEST WAY - 2 Vol
THE TWO MOORS WAY Dartmoor-Exmoor
WALKS IN KENT Bk 2
THE WEALDWAY & VANGUARD WAY

SCOTLAND
THE BORDER COUNTRY - WALKERS GUIDE
BORDER PUBS & INNS A Walker's Guide
CAIRNGORMS WINTER CLIMBS
WALKING THE GALLOWAY HILLS
THE ISLAND OF RHUM
THE SCOTTISH GLENS (Mountainbike Guide)
   Book 1:THE CAIRNGORM GLENS
   Book 2 THE ATHOLL GLENS
   Book 3 THE GLENS OF RANNOCH
SCOTTISH RAILWAY WALKS
SCRAMBLES IN LOCHABER
SCRAMBLES IN SKYE
SKI TOURING IN SCOTLAND
TORRIDON A Walker's Guide
WALKS from the WEST HIGHLAND RAILWAY
WINTER CLIMBS BEN NEVIS & GLENCOE

REGIONAL BOOKS UK & IRELAND
THE ALTERNATIVE PENNINE WAY
CANAL WALKS Vol.1: North
LIMESTONE - 100 BEST CLIMBS
THE PACKHORSE BRIDGES OF ENGLAND
THE RELATIVE HILLS OF BRITAIN
THE MOUNTAINS OF ENGLAND & WALES
   VOL 1 WALES, VOL 2 ENGLAND
THE MOUNTAINS OF IRELAND

Other guides are constantly being added to the Cicerone List.
Available from bookshops, outdoor equipment shops or direct (send s.a.e. for price list) from
CICERONE, 2 POLICE SQUARE, MILNTHORPE, CUMBRIA, LA7 7PY

CICERONE GUIDES to WALKING and CLIMBING IN FRANCE

THE BRITTANY COASTAL PATH *Alan Castle* The GR34, 360 miles around the Brittany coast takes a month to walk. Easy access from UK means it can be split into several holidays. *ISBN 1 85284 185 0*

CHAMONIX- MONT BLANC - A Walking Guide *Martin Collins* In the dominating presence of Europe's highest mountain, the scenery viewed from these walks is exceptional. Well walked paths, plenty of accommodation. *ISBN 1 85284 009 9 192pp PVC cover £8.99*

THE CORSICAN HIGH LEVEL ROUTE - Walking the GR20 *Alan Castle* The most challenging of the French LD paths - across the rocky spine of Corsica. *ISBN 1 85284 100 1 Card cover 104pp £5.99*

FRENCH ROCK *Bill Birkett* THE guide to many exciting French crags! Masses of photo topos, with selected hit-routes in detail. *ISBN 1 85284 113 3. 332pp A5 size. Card cover £14.99*

THE PYRENEAN TRAIL: GR10 *Alan Castle* The GR10 stretches from the Atlantic to the Mediterranean at a lower level than the Pyrenean High Route. Takes 50 days but is split into fortnight holiday sections. *ISBN 1 85284 038 2 184pp Card cover £7.99*

THE ROBERT LOUIS STEVENSON TRAIL *Alan Castle* 140 mile trail in the footsteps of Stevenson's "Travels with a Donkey" through the Cevennes. *ISBN 1 85284 060 9 160pp Card cover £7.99*

ROCK CLIMBS IN THE VERDON. An Introduction *Rick Newcombe*
An English-style guide, which makes for easier identification of the routes and descents. *ISBN 1 85284 015 3 72pp Card cover £5.50*

TOUR OF MONT BLANC *Andrew Harper* One of the world's best walks - the circumnavigation of the Mont Blanc massif. *ISBN 1 85284 011 0 144pp PVC cover £7.99*

TOUR OF THE OISANS: GR54 *Andrew Harper* This popular walk around the massif is similar in quality to the celebrated Tour of Mont Blanc. *ISBN 0 902363 71 9 104pp PVC cover*

THE TOUR OF THE QUEYRAS *A.Castle* A 13 day walk on the GR58 and GR541 which traverses wild but beautiful country, the sunniest part of the French Alps. This area is eminently suitable for a first Alpine visit. *ISBN 1 85284 048 X 160pp Card cover £6.99*

WALKING THE FRENCH ALPS: GR5 *Martin Collins* A guide to the popular long distance path from Lake Geneva to Nice. Split into stages, each of which could form the basis of a good holiday. *ISBN 1 85284 051 X 168pp PVC cover £8.99*

WALKING THE FRENCH GORGES *Alan Castle* 320 miles through Provence and Ardèche, includes the famous gorges of the Verdon. *ISBN 1 85284 114 1 224pp Card cover £7.99*

WALKS IN VOLCANO COUNTRY *Alan Castle* Two long distance walks in Central France- through the High Auvergne and Tour of the Velay - in a unique landscape of extinct volcanoes. *ISBN 1 85284 092 7 208pp Card cover £8.50*

THE WAY OF ST JAMES: GR65 *H.Bishop* The GR65 follows the French section of the pilgrim's route, across the Massif Central from Le Puy to the Pyrenees, in the heart of France. Full of historical associations. *ISBN 1 85284 029 3 96pp Card cover £5.50*

CICERONE GUIDES to WALKING IN SWITZERLAND
and adjacent Alpine areas

ALPINE PASS ROUTE, SWITZERLAND *Kev Reynolds* Over 15 passes along the northern edge of the Swiss Alps, past the Eiger, Jungfrau and many other renowned peaks. *ISBN 1 85284 069 2 176pp Card Cover £6.99*

THE BERNESE ALPS, SWITZERLAND *Kev Reynolds* Includes walks around Grindelwald, Lauterbrunnen and Kandersteg dominated by the great peaks of the Oberland. *ISBN 1 85284 074 9 248pp PVC cover £9.99*

CENTRAL SWITZERLAND - A Walking Guide *Kev Reynolds* A little known but delightful area stretching from Luzern to the St Gotthard, includes Engelberg and Klausen Pass. *ISBN 1 85284 131 1 216pp PVC cover £10.99*

CHAMONIX to ZERMATT The Walker's Haute Route *Kev Reynolds* The classic walk in the shadow of great peaks from Mont Blanc to the Matterhorn. *ISBN 1 85284 076 5 176pp Card cover £6.99*

WALKS IN THE ENGADINE, SWITZERLAND *Kev Reynolds* The superb country of the Bregaglia and Bernina Alps, and the National Park, are revealed for the walker. *ISBN 1 85284 003 X 192pp PVC cover £8.99*

THE JURA: WALKING THE HIGH ROUTE *Kev Reynolds* **WINTER SKI TRAVERSES** *R.Brian Evans* The High Route is a long distance path along the highest crest of the Swiss Jura. In winter the area is a paradise for walkers on cross-country skis. *ISBN 1 85284 010 2 192pp Card cover £6.99*

WALKING IN TICINO, SWITZERLAND *Kev Reynolds.* Walks in the lovely Italian part of Switzerland, surprisingly little known to British walkers. *ISBN 1 85284 098 6 184pp PVC cover £9.99*

THE VALAIS, SWITZERLAND. A Walking Guide *Kev Reynolds* The splendid scenery of the Pennine Alps, with such peaks as the Matterhorn, Dent Blanche, and Mont Rosa, providing a perfect background. *ISBN 1 85284 151 6 224pp PVC cover £11.99*

THE GRAND TOUR OF MONTE ROSA *C.J.Wright*
Vol 1 - Martigny to Valle della Sesia (via the Italian valleys) *ISBN 1 85284 177 X 250pp PVC Cover*

Vol 2 - Valle della Sesia to Martigny (via the Swiss valleys) *ISBN 1 85284 178 8 250pp* The ultimate alpine LD walk which encircles most of the Pennine Alps. *PVC Cover*

Available from bookshops, most outdoor equipment shops or direct from the publishers - please send large s.a.e for current price list

CICERONE PRESS,
2 POLICE SQUARE, MILNTHORPE,
CUMBRIA LA7 7PY
Tel: 015395 62069
Fax: 015395 63417

mountain / **sports**   **incorporating 'Mountain INFO'**

Britain's liveliest and most authorative magazine for mountaineers, climbers and ambitious hillwalkers. Gives news and commentary from the UK and worldwide, backed up by exciting features and superb colour photography.

OFFICIAL MAGAZINE

Have you read it yet?

Available monthly from your newsagent or specialist gear shop.

Call 0533 460722 for details

*BRITISH
MOUNTAINEERING
COUNCIL*

OUTDOORS
I L L U S T R A T E D

The leading all-outdoor magazine covering the active outdoors in Britain and abroad. Climbing, hiking, trekking, sailing, skiing, canoeing, diving, paragliding, travel and more. Regular features on health, equipment, photography, wildlife and environment. All in full colour throughout.

QUARTERLY   from leading newsagents

Studio 2, 114-116 Walcot Street, Bath BA1 5BG

IF YOU LIKE ADVENTUROUS ACTIVITIES ON
MOUNTAINS OR HILLS YOU WILL ENJOY

CLIMBER

& *HILLWALKER*

**MOUNTAINEERING/HILLWALKING/TREKKING
ROCK CLIMBING/SCRAMBLING IN BRITAIN
AND ABROAD**

*AVAILABLE FROM NEWSAGENTS, OUTDOOR EQUIPMENT SHOPS,
OR BY SUBSCRIPTION (6-12 MONTHS) FROM
CALEDONIAN MAGAZINES LTD, PLAZA TOWER,
EAST KILBRIDE, GLASGOW G74 1LW*

THE WALKERS' MAGAZINE

**COMPULSIVE MONTHLY READING FOR
ANYONE INTERESTED IN WALKING**

*AVAILABLE FROM NEWSAGENTS, OUTDOOR EQUIPMENT SHOPS,
OR BY SUBSCRIPTION (6-12 MONTHS) FROM
CALEDONIAN MAGAZINES LTD, PLAZA TOWER,
EAST KILBRIDE, GLASGOW G74 1LW*

Printed by CARNMOR PRINT & DESIGN
95-97 LONDON ROAD, PRESTON, LANCASHIRE, UK.